Prophetic Preaching for a Paralyzed Church

8 Sermons To Inspire Social Change

Rev. Dr. Joel Damon Taylor

Praise for
Prophetic Preaching for a Paralyzed Church

What a timely, encouraging, and enlightening word for those of us who are committed to the authentic Gospel of Jesus Christ.

— *Rev. Dr. Bartholomew Banks, President, Progressive M & E Baptist State Convention of Florida, Inc.*

Within this new age of theological thinking, where there is much emphasis on personal power, personal praise, and personal prosperity, a form of preaching has developed that seeks to pacify individualism, thereby humanizing God, deifying man, and compromising sin. However, through this publication, Dr. Taylor has set forth prudent preaching principles that speak truth to power with a view of persuasion. *Prophetic Preaching for a Paralyzed Church* will challenge all who stand in the gap between the living and the dead to passionately proclaim the truth of God's word in these times of social disorder.

— *Rev. Kenneth Maurice Davis, M. Div., President, Mississippi National Baptist State Convention*

Admittedly, the terms 'preaching' and 'paralyzed' grab attention. Dr. Joel Taylor faithfully explores the task of preaching while naming the reality of the ears that hear it. He, not unlike Moses, realizes that the task of leading God's people out of Egypt also involves getting "Egypt" out of the people. It is no secret that context challenges homiletical skills in various ways, with each context having a stubborn particularity. Prophetic preaching dares to suggest to paralyzed or satisfied ears that God is still speaking in the midst of the paralysis.

— Dr. Ozzie Smith, Adjunct Professor of Ministry & D. Min. Advisor, McCormick Theological Seminary

...Dr. Taylor issues a compelling challenge to those who carry the gospel in its most relevant form by making a profound argument that the most effectual means of securing the continuance of our social, civil, and religious liberties is always to remember with reverence and gratitude the source from which they flow.

— Rev. Stephen Thurston, M. Div., 14th President, National Baptist Convention of America International, Inc.

This book provides a biblical antidote for the paralysis gripping churches in the non-social action mode. Dr. Taylor demonstrates the role preaching the Bible has in transformation as the Word becomes flesh. This pre-test and post-test sermon model can become a template for pastors around the world who seek to measure prophetic proclamation's impact on congregations.

— Rev. Samuel C. Tolbert Jr., M. Div., 15th President, National Baptist Convention of America International, Inc.

Acknowledgments

I extend a heartfelt thanks to the St. Paul Missionary Baptist Church, where I have had the privilege to serve as pastor for over thirty years to preach about social activism. I also thank the Greater Mt. Pleasant Missionary Baptist Church, who simultaneously extended to me the unique privilege to serve as their pastor over ten years ago. I am most thankful to the members, past and present, who have shared with me as contextual associates on this project. Thank you: Kimberly Brownfield, Jacqueline Baylis, Samuel Conner, DeShaise Green, Barbara Hankins, Emma Harper, Minnie Nunn, Seabron Phillips, and Dorothy Snow. Your assistance will never be forgotten.

Special thanks to my two mentors on this journey. I started this project struggling because my father never heard me preach. I am completing it with two blessings: Dr. George E. McRae and Dr. Leah Gaskin Fitchue, a father and a mother in the ministry.

Special thanks to all of the Fitchue-McRae Fellows who also shared this journey with me.

Many thanks to all of the consultants who have shared their bountiful knowledge on this tedious journey. Thank you: Dr. Frank Thomas, Dr. Alan Ragland, Dr. Ozzie Smith, and Dr. Joan Hill. I could not have made it without your moral and spiritual support.

Thank you, Dr. Roland Womack, for encouraging me to go back to school. Thank you, Rev. Maurice Davis, for all of your prayers and phone calls along this journey. Thank you, Dr. Wyatt Tee Walker, for sharing your theological insights with me. Thank you, Mrs. Betty Simpson, for your help in editing.

Special thanks to my family. Thanks to my brothers, Alden and J. J., for being there in your own way. Thanks to all of my aunts and uncles and grandmothers who still serve God. Thank you to the late Reverend and Mrs. J. P. White, my father-in-law and mother-in-law, for all your support with the "three children" and words of encouragement.

Thank you, my children, Jessica and Rev. Jasper, for being the joy of my life on this journey. Last but not least, thank you, Cynthia, my wife and best friend, for all your patience as well as your spiritual and moral support.

I dedicate this book to the late Rev. J. J. Taylor, Sr., and Johnnie Taylor, my parents, who now reside on the other side of the Jordan River. Thank you, Mom and Dad, for instilling within me the love of God. Without your training and guidance, this project would never have materialized.

CONTENTS

Foreword

Preaching a prophetic message of social activism suffocates outside of a specific venue and concrete context. George A. Buttrick sounded the right note: "All preaching is venue specific." Dr. Taylor presents you with a book that not only visits the halls of the academy but sets you down on the street corners of Englewood, Illinois. This is no detached review by a sociologist but the passionate proclamation of a prophet fastened to his own venue.

In so doing, Taylor gives another context, that of the influences in his life and ministry. As Fred Craddock noted, it is always right to ask someone where he got his ears. That is the constellation of those who shaped his preaching. He also sets his soundly in a theological context. Preaching is a profoundly theological act.

Sermons must move from *then* to *now* to effect change. Taylor takes you from a valley of dry bones in Mesopotamia to the streets of Englewood. There becomes here. Then becomes now. This book does not hold a memorial service for the passages preached but rather presents them as living, embodied truth.

It is a commonplace that those who wrote Scripture wrote it not from a place of privilege but from the margins. We are now recognizing that its best interpreters are those who deal with life on the margins. The words spoken long ago in another world come to life in this book and walk up and down the streets of Chicagoland. And yet, because they are specifically somewhere, they are, therefore, everywhere. Generalities alone beget generalities. Specifics stick to anywhere.

Dr. Joel C. Gregory
Holder of the George W. Truett Endowed Chair in Preaching and Evangelism at George W. Truett Theological Seminary of Baylor University

About This Book

This book recounts an effort designed to address the issue of apathy in social activism among the members of the St. Paul Missionary Baptist Church in Chicago, Illinois. Eight sermons, preached from texts in Ezekiel, Isaiah, Amos, and Philippians, were designed to solicit a social action response. A quantitative pretest and post-test questionnaire documented the results. These results were further documented by a ministry sign-up project at the end of the process. The results indicate that the congregation has grown in the area of social activism.

The Power of the Pulpit

It is a divine-human enterprise and is properly concerned with the whole of life. Concern with social crises is not simply permissible in preaching: it is imperative. This is no elective course, no peripheral concern of the Christian gospel. It is its major thrust. Without it preaching is weak and anemic and is hardly worth the name. Authentic preaching takes into account the social issues and dilemmas that plague the human family. It is sensitive to the relevancy of the Christian gospel for these concerns and it proclaims that relevancy.[1] — **Kelly Miller Smith**

Preachers stand weekly before various congregations, expounding on God's Holy Word. Down through the years, the pulpit has been viewed as the place where God meets His people through the preached word delivered by His spokesperson. In the African American community, it is said that the preacher is one of the most powerful persons as he or she stands weekly in the pulpit to share words of hope, inspiration, peace, and love to those that come to listen. Initially, I ran from preaching, but now I have accepted my call, and I am grateful that I have the privilege to preach. With this calling came many areas that interested me as a preacher.

First and foremost, I was concerned about the power of the pulpit. I have witnessed some preachers stand and preach and when they finish, the listeners are motivated to take on the world. On the other hand, I have observed some preachers stand with a wonderfully rich and extensive vocabulary and expound the text eloquently, but when they finish, the listeners feel that they have merely been given a lecture. The message has given the listeners no inspiration to react or respond to social issues in the immediate future.

This is one of the reasons that I became concerned with this project; I deem it pertinent that preaching should address social issues. Moreover, I believe it is imperative that somehow social problems and dilemmas be dealt with from the pulpit. As a researcher, my goal is to seek ways and means that can help me motivate my congregation to become socially active. When I accepted my call into the ministry, I vowed not to become a preacher that failed to deal with social problems in the preaching of the gospel.

In addition, I realized that my pastorate had not given meaning to the popular statement, "We come to church to worship, and we depart to serve." We were having a great experience every Sunday in our worship service, but I realized that something was missing. Our worship service had become just an activity, and it did not move those who played a part in the church and community of faith to become people of action. I felt, therefore, that my preaching was encouraging social passivism and that somehow I needed to develop sermons that inspired social activism.

I believed that preaching could make a difference in the St. Paul Missionary Baptist. After I encountered apathy in social activism among the congregation, I embarked on a journey to test my conviction that preaching should lead the people to be socially active in the church as well as the community. I set out on this pilgrimage in order to analyze how preaching of the word from biblical texts would affect my congregation. This book details what transpired in the planning and implementation of this project, which was previously titled "Biblical Preaching That Establishes the Norm for Social Activism."

Chapter 1 covers my personal life as seen in my life, calling, and ministry. It also describes my context, the St. Paul Missionary Baptist Church, where I have served as pastor for over thirty years. It encapsulates my gift of preaching and the problem of social activism in the church, which become a synergy for Kingdom building.

Chapter 2 explores the literature that I have reviewed and which has become beneficial and foundational to this project. Since this project deals with preaching, some major works authored by pastors have been critically analyzed. This chapter also includes relevant helpful literature. Lastly, this section presents books that discuss social ministries and document their effectiveness.

Chapter 3 highlights the ultimate focus and theological framework for this project. In this section, I lift up a definition of preaching and highlight certain key theological aspects of God, the prophets, and Jesus in relation to social activism. This chapter also candidly unfolds with people, pastors, and churches who have influenced me with their examples of social activism.

Chapter 4 presents the eight sermons in the "Operation Restoration" series. These sermons were designed to motivate the congregation to social activism and persuade members to address some social issues.

In the conclusion, I summarize and reflect on the project. I highlight the positive aspects and examine some limitations I encountered. I also offer suggestions for future studies in biblical preaching.

CHAPTER ONE

You Can Run,
But You Can't Hide

God never calls a person without giving that person a
specific assignment; a place to carry out the assignment;
and the amazing grace needed to complete the mission
assigned.[2] — **Harold Carter**

Harold Carter's words were never truer than as seen
in the story of Jonah. Jonah realized that God had called
him to go preach to the Ninevites, but he was hardheaded
and refused to heed God's powerful call. Jonah didn't
want to do what God commanded him to do because of
his prejudice toward the Gentiles. Jonah represents many
ministers who recognize the powerful call from God to
preach the gospel but initially reject Him. Many do not
obey God's command at first; they try to run from God
like Jonah did.

> *But Jonah rose up to flee unto Tarshish from the presence of the LORD, and went down to Joppa; and he found a ship going to Tarshish: so he paid the fare thereof, and went down into it, to go with them unto Tarshish from the presence of the LORD.* — ***Jonah 1:3 (KJV)***

God had given Jonah a directive to go to Nineveh and deliver a message to the people, but he was reluctant to go and carry out the directive that God gave him. I, like many others, see a reflection of myself in Jonah, for like Jonah, I ran from God. It was only later that I learned that we, as called-out people of God, can run away from God, but we cannot hide. Ultimately, God will get our attention.

It is ironic that I, Joel Damon Taylor, would embark upon a project on "Prophetic Preaching for a Paralyzed Church" because I fought my calling to the ministry for many years. Reflecting on my life, however, I can see how the hand of God touched me, brought me out of hiding, and led me to become pastor of St. Paul Missionary Baptist Church.

I now live to preach God's Holy Word. How did I evolve to become a gospel preacher? What steps did I take in order to arrive at this juncture in life? Where did it all begin? I want to share some important insights about my life that led me to accept my call as a gospel preacher. I also wish to share how God led me to become the pastor of St. Paul and how He has directed me to lead this church to become socially active.

Early Life and Family

Without reservation, I believe that God has a purpose for our lives from the very beginning of our inceptive existence. I was born on August 6, 1963, in Chicago, Illinois, at a historical landmark, Provident Hospital. I am the second of three sons born to the union of the late Reverend Jasper Joseph Taylor, Sr., and Johnnie P. Taylor. My elder brother is Alden Darrell Taylor, and my younger brother is Jasper Joseph Taylor, Jr. My family was one in which values, morals, and the fear of God were taught daily.

As I think about my late parents, I believe that it was their spirituality that laid the foundation for my brothers and me. Both of my parents were reared in the South, where they had strong religious upbringings. My father's southern roots brought into focus my late grandfather, Rev. Jim Taylor. My grandfather had served as a deacon for many years prior to becoming a pastor of a Baptist church. His religious ways of life, as well as the hardworking values that he instilled in my father, were passed on to me.

In many instances during this project, I saw, in more ways than I ever dreamed of, how those values have influenced my life. The more I reflect upon them, the more I see my ministry and me. I am quick to say that much of my ministry seems to be like a "chip off the old block." The faith of my father and grandfather was pivotal for me because they taught it to me and demonstrated it to me in their daily lives. When I think back on their precepts and examples, I can see how their views on helping people and their diligent efforts at trying to make a viable difference in society planted in me a desire to become a social activist. I acknowledge that their values, principles, and ideals are still alive because they live within me and manifest themselves in everything I undertake in the ministry for the Lord.

Family Setting

My parents, Jasper Joseph and Johnnie Pearl, were married while my father was the youthful pastor of the New Home Baptist Church in Leighton, Alabama. They moved to Chicago to the Englewood area in the early 1960s when my father was called to pastor the St. Paul Missionary Baptist Church. My father provided for our family's daily needs through his financial means of support as a pastor and through his craft as a general contractor while my mother took care of the daily operations of the home. I was blessed, especially during my formative years, to have both of my parents in the home. They did not send us to church; they carried us. Often I recall one of my father's favorite phrases: "Everyone who lives in this house under this roof will go to the church house, or they will find another place to stay." Later, I learned that my father mimicked this phrase to us because it was also said to him as a child.

In my early childhood years, my life was filled with sundry church activities. Since it was mandated that I go to church as a child, I thought that when I became older and could make decisions for myself, I would not want to have anything to do with the church. In fact, as I reflect now, I believe this period of my life was the beginning of my attempt to run away from the call to the ministry. Nevertheless, when I was nine years of age, a substantive experience occurred with my accepting Christ as my personal savior. I was baptized at the St. Paul Baptist Church, where my father pastored, and I became active in church activities. It was at this point in my life that my interest in the study of the Word of God surfaced. However, I kept this interest secret from everyone.

Running from God

Now, it is easy for me to see how, as a young man, I was fighting the truth and running from my call to preach the gospel while others could readily see God's hand upon me. I have vivid memories of the words of one man in particular, the late Deacon Arthur Johnson, who consistently said to me, "Young man, you have been called to preach; you should accept your calling." My constant immediate response was, "No way!" Also, I discovered later that my father and his close friend, the late Reverend Dalton Nunn, had many conversations about God's call on my life.

But saying "yes" to God was difficult for me. At that time, I had a problem with the notion of becoming a preacher because I felt that I was unfairly treated as a preacher's child. I believed that I was treated differently from other children because I was the "preacher's kid." I recall that whenever a group of us children were mischievous, I was always singled out as the one who should not have done wrong. Consequently, I became bitter, and I did not want to serve these so-called Christians. In addition to being pressured about my conduct as a preacher's kid, it appeared to me that the people who had a problem with my father transferred their feelings and took out their frustrations on me.

Moreover, my church life involved taking part in activities against my will. Before and during adolescence, I found myself singing in the choir, not because I had a magnificent singing voice or because I wanted to sing but because my parents wanted me to do it. In spite of not having a melodious voice, often I stood before the congregation, singing various songs that I did not want to sing. No way did I want to preach!

Along with making me sing, my parents, obviously believing me to be musically inclined or desiring to resurrect some musical inclination, enrolled me in music school to learn to play the organ. I hated this with a passion. Subsequently, they pushed me to become a musician for the Sunday school. I did not want to play the organ because of the stigma associated with male organists. The male organist was stereotyped or labeled by the community as a "homosexual." I knew that I was not a homosexual and did not want to be labeled as such.

Thinking that music would be a great career for me, my parents invested a large sum of money in a Hammond organ. This musical career was short-lived, and I was able to persuade my parents to allow me to halt this musical talent search. Looking back, however, I feel that even then, through the spiritual music, God was attempting to bring me closer to Him, yet I was running farther away.

Chasing My Own Dreams

I had my agenda for my life, and surely God had His. My dream was to become a professional baseball shortstop with a major league team like the Los Angeles Dodgers. I played baseball from the time I was a "little leaguer" until my senior high school year. Baseball was an outlet for me, and I was a good player. Because of my insatiable desire to play this sport, my playing skills, and my aspirations to be a major league team player, I worked hard to make this dream become a reality.

But, at the tender age of twelve, I felt the call to preach. At this young age, I asked God to allow me to play baseball and promised, "One day I will preach for You." As much as I loved baseball, it seemed that one day, suddenly all of the joy, love, and excitement that I once felt for the game was removed, along with all of my skills. In short, I found that I was no longer content with baseball. The opportunity was presented to me for a scholarship from Lewis University, but God had other plans for my future, and they did not include baseball. Being a professional baseball player was my own agenda, not God's.

Continuing to run from God as an older teen, I pivoted my interests. I decided that I would become a lawyer. I had always enjoyed Perry Mason and the Matlock on television, and I felt that I could be like them. So, I enrolled in the pre-law program at DePaul

University in Chicago, Illinois. Through the school career service, I secured employment at a law firm, and I felt that I was on my way to becoming an efficient attorney. Initially, however, I was undecided in my area of concentration in the liberal arts program, so I chose religious studies as my major. Still operating in the denial mode as far as my call to the ministry was concerned, I thought that if I were not successful in law, I would just "teach" religion. I was unaware that all the time I was drawing closer to my calling. God was at work. He was moving all of the obstacles out of my life, making the pathway straight, and cutting deep channels in my life for His will to flow through.

Accepting My Calling

One Sunday morning, while I was riding in the car with my father en route to Sunday school, he noticed a book that I was reading entitled *Understanding Religious Life*. With a strange look in his eyes, he asked, "Why are you reading this book?" I answered that I was reading it for a class at school. Later, I saw him looking through the book with a smile on his face; it was then that I discovered he had knowledge of my call to preach. My father made no comment, and I am sure that this was because he did not want to influence my decision. He wanted God to lead me in the direction that I should go. My biggest regret is that my father died before he had a chance to hear me preach. Nevertheless, I rest assured that he knew I could run from God only for a short while.

In 1982, something happened that changed my life forever. On Friday, October 29, my father was murdered on the wicked streets of Chicago! I was devastated. His death affected me unlike anything that I had experienced up to that point in my life. My father was my idol, my role model, my mentor, and he was gone. He had passed from transient life into eternal life to be with the Lord. His death, rather than pulling me closer to the Lord, pushed me further away. I was angry with God, and like we do at times of hurt and dismay, I questioned Him: "How could You allow this to happen to my father? How could You take away a good man and leave all of the unrighteous, unreligious, and unsaved people here on earth?"

In the midst of the devastation of my father's death, I encountered another crisis. It appeared that the church people who had been so supportive of us as a family seemed to change overnight. I felt like totally disassociating myself with the church because so many surfaced as hypocrites. Feeling hurt, depressed, broken-hearted and devastated, I continued to run from God.

The next few years became even more difficult for me. My life was falling apart. I tried to turn to worldly pleasures, and I became a violent person full of anger and rage, but God continued to call me. Every time I went to church, I heard the call of God. Every time I went home and went to sleep, I heard the call of God. No matter where I went, I heard the call of God. No matter how bad, tough, and crazy I acted, I could still hear the call of God.

Then, on the fourth Sunday in September 1984, I attended morning worship service at St. Paul Missionary Baptist Church. That Sunday morning, Reverend Milton Brunson, Pastor of Christ Tabernacle Baptist Church of Chicago, Illinois, delivered the message. Something happened to me during that delivery. The Holy Spirit made His move in my life. At the end of the sermon, I stood with tears in my eyes and came forth to announce to the congregation and the world that I was accepting my calling to preach the gospel. I had run long enough, and I could not run or hide anymore. It was time to accept the calling on my life.

At the age of twenty-one, on November 25, 1984, at 7:00 p.m., I preached my initial sermon. It was entitled "Is There a God?" Preaching this sermon, for me, was like releasing the cap on a vacuum and allowing all the pressure to escape. God began to manifest His will in my life. Then, on March 31, 1985, I was called to pastor the St. Paul Missionary Baptist Church, where my late father had pastored, and in April of the same year, I was ordained. I had been running from God when He had such wonderful things in store for my life the whole time. Preaching truly was God's calling on my life.

My Family

As I sat in the pulpit on March 25, 1985, waiting to deliver my initial sermon, a young lady walked down the aisle with her mother and sat next to my mother. Her name was Cynthia Vernice White. This was the young lady whose hair I had pulled while we were children growing up. Her father, Pastor of the Greater Mt. Pleasant Missionary Baptist Church (providentially the church where I also serve as Pastor), had been affiliated with the St. Paul Church and a friend of my family for all of our lives. But as this young lady came down the aisle that day, I felt in my heart that I heard a voice say, "She will be your wife." And she is.

On August 23, 1986, Cynthia Vernice White and I were joined together in holy matrimony. I am eternally thankful for this special gift that God has given to me. My wife, having grown up as a preacher's daughter, understands many of the trials and tribulations that ministers have to experience. In addition, God gave her two great musical gifts. She is a wonderful vocalist and a talented musician. God could not have provided me with a more wonderful partner to share my life and complement my ministry.

God continued to bless our union by giving us two wonderful and energetic children: a son, Rev. Jasper Paul, and a daughter, Jessica Dominique. I could not have asked for a more ideal family. Oftentimes, when I look at my children, I think about the plight of other young children who are not as blessed as mine. It makes me want to preach this gospel of social activism even more. I preach about the family, for I realize the significance and value of the family as the first basic institution in society. The very fiber of the family structure is in trouble today. Through the message of the gospel and through social activism, however, a change will come.

Education

My father always taught my brothers and me that training and preparation are required to succeed in life. Because of this important instruction and guidance, I was insistent that I must continue to matriculate in institutions of higher learning. I received my Bachelor of Arts degree in Religious Studies from DePaul University in 1988. My hungering and thirsting for knowledge then led me to the Northern Baptist Theological Seminary in Lombard, Illinois. By God's grace, I graduated from Northern on June 5, 1993, earning a Master of Divinity degree with a specialization in pastoral ministry.

The desire to continue my education persisted, and I graduated with my Doctor of Ministry Degree from United Theological Seminary of Dayton, Ohio, in 1998. It is no mistake that I chose Social Activism as my preaching project, for this truly exemplifies my call in ministry. While I once attempted to run and hide from God, I now take joy and pleasure in trying to be available and accessible to God as an instrument to be utilized in bringing about social change.

Gifts

It is a wonderful experience to know God's will for my life and an even more wonderful experience to recognize the gifts that God has given me. One gift that God has given me is to preach the gospel. I have never wanted to be an average preacher; I always wanted to be one who is trained and specialized in ministry. It is ironic that I spent years running from preaching and now find that preaching has become one of the joys of my life. The more I preach, the more I want to preach. Years ago, it was not fulfilling to me to go to church all of the time, but now I am always looking for a spiritually motivating service of which I can be a part. I recognize my gift to expound the Word of God, to spread the good news about Jesus Christ, and to deliver a sermon in such a way that hearts, minds, and lives will be changed.

I thank God, too, for the gift of service, for being able to serve the people and community where I pastor. I've been gifted to prepare and preach a message every week that will make a difference in the parishioners and lead them to higher heights for the glory of God. My gifts have come from God to serve this present age, my calling to fulfill. I believe that the Lord gave me these gifts to serve the church and community where He planted me as pastor, preacher, and teacher.

The Place

The church that I primarily serve is located in Chicago, Illinois, one of the largest metropolitan cities in the United States of America. Chicago has gained a dual reputation. It is said to be one of the best cities in which to live as well as one of the worst cities in which to live. Chicago is known as the "windy city" because of its bone-piercing and chilling winds that travel at high velocities, having no respect for people or things. From the Al Capone era up until this present day, Chicago has maintained another reputation of being a city of crime, corruption, and chaos.

Although Chicago is integrated, it is still a city that is racially and ethnically polarized and economically separated. One of the areas in the city is Englewood, a community located on the south side of Chicago. Englewood has become one of the undesirable communities in the Chicago land area because it is known as a "cesspool for violence." It has a high crime rate and heavy drug trafficking, and it is plagued by gangs.

According to the 1990 census, there were only 48,434 people living in Englewood. Of these residents, 48,027 were of African American descent, with the only other race of any significance being the 224 whites who live in the community. According to the same 1990 census report, the average income was $13,243 per household while in the entire Chicago area the average income was $26,301 per household. For a better picture of the household income in Englewood, these figures indicate that rather than an increase in income since 1979, there was a decrease in the income:

> Today the unemployment rate in Englewood is more than 18 percent. The number of housing units has dropped from 28,000 to 19,000 in the last decade, and one in eight residents live in overcrowded conditions. The dependency rate is high, 40 percent are less than 18 years old and females head more than half of the households with children less than 18. The median family income is among the lowest in the city and more than a third of all the residents live in poverty. The median value of owner

occupied homes in Englewood is among the 10 lowest in the city.[3]

What startles me as I reflect on these statistics from 1990 is that since then very little has changed. In fact, due to the state of Chicago, many of the inhabitants of Englewood have either died or left Chicago altogether. According to the 2010 census (twenty years later), there were 30,654 residents.[4] My assumption is that the nearly 18,000 inhabitants of Englewood have either left by choice or gentrification or are now deceased due to natural or violent causes.

What becomes clear is that Englewood is and has been a place for ministry because it lacks positive role models of both the male and female gender. The young people are struggling in the midst of an environment that seeks to destroy them. In this community, many youths are losing and destroying their lives by making the wrong choices. This is a place where our young people have given their lives to gangs, violence, and teenage pregnancy and are dropping out of high school.

The educational system in this community is substandard. Two of the high schools in Englewood, namely Roberson and Englewood, are on probation. As a result of substandard education, the ratio is low for the development and production of intelligent black Americans who can successfully matriculate at the college level and ultimately make a viable contribution to society.

Undoubtedly, sin and Satan run rampant in Englewood, having a devastating effect on the residents.

In the midst of this community, however, is the St. Paul Missionary Baptist Church, which stands as a beacon light.

The History of St. Paul Missionary Baptist Church

The St. Paul Missionary Baptist Church was organized in 1919 in another African American community north of Englewood called the "gap area." Since its organization, St. Paul has been faced with many obstacles. In 1922, after only a few years of existence, the church membership disbanded, but it was reorganized one year later. Between 1923 and 1997, St. Paul was pastored by eight different ministers.

Despite the early problems, the church began to move forward in a positive direction under the leadership of the late Reverend J. H. Irwin, a mover, who served from 1937 until 1962. It was under his leadership that many of the boards and auxiliaries were formed. During Reverend Irwin's tenure, St. Paul relocated from the "gap area' at 45th and St. Lawrence Avenue to its present location at 6954 South Union Avenue in the Englewood community.

In April of 1962, my late father, Rev. J. J. Taylor, Sr., became the pastor of St. Paul. Under his leadership, the St. Paul Missionary Baptist Church was extended and remodeled. During this extensive renovation project, I realized that my father was a social activist. Social activism was his life. After completing the series of sermons in my model, I realized that many of my father's dreams were left unfulfilled because of his tragic death. Building a church to reach the community was Pastor J. J. Taylor's dream.

The extension he initiated to the church included a community service center, which was the site of a gymnasium and a day-care facility. In addition to the community center, my father was responsible for the construction of a sixty-unit apartment building that provided decent housing for low-income families in the church as well as the rest of the community. The building was owned and operated by the church for many years.

The untimely death of Pastor Taylor in 1982 prevented him from making his complete vision of ministry a reality at St. Paul. In fact, his sudden death momentarily destroyed the vision of ministry in the church membership. I realize today, however, that my father's model of ministry is the same model and vision that God has given me.

The death of Pastor J. J. Taylor left St. Paul without a pastor for one year before Reverend Willie Jackson was called to serve in 1983. The calling of Reverend Jackson was controversial for St. Paul and created a separation among the parishioners. Hence, the church split. Rev. Jackson's pastorate at St. Paul was short-lived. He stayed at the helm of the church for less than one year. In August of 1994, Reverend Jackson elected to resign from the leadership of the St. Paul Missionary Baptist Church to organize another church. This led to the second split in the St. Paul family.

These two divisions had serious repercussions for the ministry of the St. Paul family spiritually, physically, and financially. Accordingly, the split damaged the vision of St. Paul. This left the church in the maintenance mode of ministry, with members responsible for keeping the doors of the church open.

The fellowship and love among the members remaining at St. Paul was damaged, as well as the love between families and friends who opted to leave. Despite the strife, the congregation endured. It was time to elect a new leader. God had been busy preparing me, a young man, to become the shepherd for His flock, who had been through a very difficult experience.

In April of 1985, I was elected pastor of the St. Paul Missionary Baptist Church. The congregation was receptive to my position as the leader of the flock. When I became pastor, the membership began to look to me for leadership from God for their ministry, mandate, and mission. I realize that because of the confidence they have placed in me, I am accountable for the good and the bad during my pastorate. My goal is to develop a Christian community within the church that will make a difference, not only for the congregation but also for the Englewood community.

Problems

As I looked at my context, which is the St. Paul congregation and community, I realized that the problem is apathy toward social activism. When I became pastor, according to our church records, we had 939 members on our church roll. There is strength in numbers, and this is a positive aspect for any church. But even with the positive membership number, there was a problem. I realized that there were 939 Christians just going through the motions.

The majority of these 939 persons were part of a group or auxiliary within the church whose main purpose was to raise money. For this reason, most of their time and energy was expended in fundraising to help keep the church financially afloat. Camaraderie and fellowship are important in groups and auxiliaries as support systems, but in spite of the good I saw, I realized that the membership needed to be more actively involved in social change. There was a void. I saw the need for the membership to become socially active in repairing the breaches in the church and in the community.

Our services have always been powerfully inspiring and educational. Prayer, preaching, and praise have always been strong components in our worship experience. Since our worship service is expressive and explosive, oftentimes praise is rendered in a charismatic manner with dancing and shouting. We have a tremendous, spirit-filled worship service each Sunday, but I have become concerned that when the members leave the church, they do not involve themselves in those things that would truly make a difference in the world. It is my hope that through this project, our church will be moved to "depart to serve" and become a beacon light for all the community to see. I sincerely believe that God is calling the Christian community not only to have fellowship but also to have active discipleship by making a difference in the world.

The teaching ministry of our church is very effective. Every Sunday before morning worship services, the members of the congregation attend Sunday school classes to learn the Word of God. Through the Sunday school, teaching techniques have been developed to minister effectively to all age groups. In addition to Sunday school, St. Paul has an extensive teaching ministry on Wednesday evenings. It begins with individual Mission and Bible study classes that are structured to educate members of all teaching ministries, and it culminates with a church-wide Bible study and prayer service.

I believe that heretofore the congregation's problem was that they were studying and reading the Word of God and learning from the Word, but they were not applying concepts and precepts to daily living or becoming involved with social issues. However, I believe that the Word of God leads us to become socially active.

One of the key factors to solving our problem of social activism in St. Paul is the need for perpetual financing. Although the church has grown in financial strength, there is still a need for more committed financial support from the membership. This is still one of the most pressing needs for any congregation located in an urban area. In order to operate effectively and efficiently, the ministry needs adequate financial support.

I fully believe that the church should be supported according to biblical mandates, which include tithes, offerings, and sacrificial gifts. As previously stated, church auxiliaries were primarily concerned with the financial support of the church through fundraising. In St. Paul, this method has changed. I strongly encourage the membership to put God first in everything they do; this includes giving from their pocketbooks. Continual preaching, teaching, and encouraging of fundamental biblical principles on giving will help to solve the financial problem.

In most instances, within my context, people are willing to give and contribute to make a vision become a reality when they fully understand the vision. I have come to realize that if the members know that they can use their resources to bring about social activism, they will be willing to invest to make a difference. Because they want to make a difference, they are willing not only to look out for themselves but also to look out for others.

Using My Gift

My goal was to make our church a more holistic church and utilize the gift that God has given me to instill in the hearts and minds of the membership of St. Paul the desire to become more socially active. I have used my gift of preaching the gospel so that the church where I serve will "enter to worship and depart to serve." My goal has been and continues to be to deliver biblical preaching that produces the norm of social activism. I have been called to preach, and I understand more than ever before the necessity of preaching sermons that can change hearts, lives, and behavior. If the church that I serve is really going to make a difference, the Word of God must truly touch the people and bring about change.

I believe the social activism that God is calling our church to be a part of will occur when the people of God demonstrate a willingness to become socially active. Their understanding of the vision and willingness to work can be achieved through preaching. This book includes eight sermons that I preached at the St. Paul Missionary Baptist Church that inspired social change.

Whatever God calls you to do, learn from me that you can run but you cannot hide. As God's chosen pastor, vessel, preacher, and servant, I had to accept and embrace my calling to make a difference in the setting where I minister. Jonah preached, and the whole town of Nineveh repented and turned back to God. I have preached and will continue to preach messages that will inspire people to be change agents and become socially active. God can use anyone to make a difference in the lives of the poor, sick, afflicted, disabled, oppressed, disenfranchised, hurt, hopeless, and enslaved.

Since I preached these messages, God has been using the St. Paul Church to help the community in practical ways. We began a tutoring program for students in need of extra teaching. It is an after-school program implemented through an elementary school adopted by St. Paul, which is one block from our church. We held a mentoring program for the young boys and girls of our church and in the surrounding community. We have used our gymnasium to minister to the total man and woman.

In addition, we have a feeding and clothing program. The apex of my dream will be to relaunch a community day-care facility and build low-income housing and an elderly care shelter. This building program will create jobs as well as teach people how to prepare for jobs.

By using my gift of prophetic preaching, my desire is to continue to lead this church as a healer, helper, and hope from the Word of God in this community. My aim is to effect social change through preaching that will encourage the members to be more willing to give to those who are in need and inspire them to become excited about being able to give and help the less fortunate in our community and in foreign lands. I have made my choice as a preacher. Motivated by Miles Jerome Jones, I choose to continue to "create a sermon with the expectation that such a personal statement of faith will move from utterance to action."[5]

Chapter 1 Notes

_____

_____

_____

_____

_____

_____

_____

_____

_____

_____

_____

_____

_____

_____

_____

_____

_____

_____

_____

_____

_____

_____

_____

_____

Standing on Tall Shoulders

If every community had a team of preachers who kept the tone of the good news before the people with relevant, timely preaching, keeping Jesus alive before them, letting the historical Jesus of Galilee, Judea, and Perea walk before them, and the risen Christ of the ages inspire and strengthen them, while lifting up those conditions that the good news exposes and seeks to redeem, the churches would reflect the tone of the good news of God.[6] — **Samuel D. Proctor**

A good sermon is a direct personal address, individual consultation on a group scale intended to achieve results. In whatever way the sermons theme may first be suggested, it must, early in the process, present to the preacher an object to be obtained, a result to be worked for, a definite purpose to whose fulfillment everything he says will be directed. Aimless preaching, whether in exposition of texts or discussion of subjects, is the pulpit's curse.[7] — **Harry Emerson Fosdick**

The preacher that stands weekly has a tremendous job in proclaiming the Word of God globally. Many people who make up congregations come to church weekly, looking for answers to many of the problems that have bogged them down in life. In the African American community, the preachers in the pulpit have generally been persons of influence in the lives of the individuals who hear them expound the Word each and every week.

Whenever I think of the past, I can see a preacher standing in the gap, speaking for God to the congregation with a message of hope for them all. When I think of our future, I believe that it will take powerful preaching from the pulpit to move people toward a higher plateau in service for the Lord. This motivation must come from the person who preaches the Word of God with persuasion. Three questions arise:

- Is there a method that should be used?
- Is there a certain style that should be used?
- What authors and scholars have spoken on this subject, and what did they say?

I strongly believe that preaching from the pulpit can and will move the people of God to be socially active. The preacher must seek out and use methods that will motivate the congregation. As Fosdick suggests, preaching should not be aimless. I feel that preaching must be done with purpose. The preacher's motive each and every week should be to deliver a message with a purpose to the congregation at large. Each message should be directed toward a specific goal that the preacher is hoping to achieve with the help of the Lord. If the pastor and people are to be jointly productive, the preaching must be inspiring and motivational enough to cause the people to want to produce.

Preaching must be done with an aim to meet the needs of the Christians that make up the community of faith as well as the needs of the community in which the church rests. I believe that in many pulpits around the country, preachers stand and preach without any aim. Many have not reached the people of God with relevant and timely messages. To paraphrase Fosdick, preaching to meet a need focuses on an object to be obtained, the results to be worked for, and the purpose to be directed.

The aim of preaching to the masses should be to address the problematic conditions that Christians and congregations must face. As Proctor suggests, the pastor needs to have on his mind and heart preaching that is timely and relevant. Pastors should aim at some of the conditions that the Word of God lifts up in the Holy Scripture. In aiming at some of these conditions, pastors must first rectify or redeem the situation at hand. This type of preaching does not only talk about the problem but also renders solutions by placing God in the puzzle.

It is my belief that preaching can produce the norm for social activism, leading individuals to work toward making things better for the poor, sick, handicapped, oppressed, disenfranchised, hurt, hopeless, and enslaved. As one considers the many works and efforts made on preaching with purpose for social change, it becomes clear that any new ideas stand on tall shoulders.

One of the major texts for this model was a book written by Dr. Samuel D. Proctor entitled *Preaching about Crisis in the Community*. This book is important for many different reasons but most importantly for the messages and the method of preaching given in the last chapter. Dr. Proctor highlights certain information that can be most helpful. He suggests that there are certain priorities that need to be eliminated when one is preaching in crisis communities.

Some issues that were a part of my preaching model of eight sermons had to deal with the problems of poverty, education, and the family structure. The idea is that the whole community needs to be affected by living water, even those who are on the low end of the economic spectrum. Based on the gospel of Jesus, caring for those who experience hopeless, hurting, and hindered lives has become a life mission for me and the St. Paul congregation where I serve. Dr. Proctor has made me more aware that the pulpit needs to address the issues of crisis and not only label them but also suggest means for solutions.

The model of preaching recommended by Dr. Proctor is a key to the model of the sermons that I preached. The method of preaching he recommends is the dialectical method of sermon construction. This method comes from the German Georg Wilhelm Friedrich Hegel. It affords pastors the opportunity to preach messages that will bless the congregation by preaching with an aim. Dr. Proctor presents the following outline for the dialectical sermon construction:

- **Subject**

- **Proposition**

- **Text**

  Introduction (antithesis), the real.

  Transition (thesis), the ideal.

  Relevant question to reconcile the real and the ideal.

  Body (synthesis), the message, the resolution which answers the relevant question in two or three or four or perhaps as many as five or six points.[8]

This outline was helpful with other ideas or methods that were added.

This dialectical method was expanded in Proctor's other book, *The Certain Sound of the Trumpet: Crafting a Sermon of Authority.* He expands this method of preaching with a chapter on each movement of the outline. According to Proctor, this method of preaching "will introduce and sustain people in a fulfilling religious experience, a relationship with God that enhances every dimension of life, and a discipleship to Jesus that provides a paradigm for the daily application and praxis of that relationship."[9] This method was used as a basis of preaching the eight sermons in the series, but other authors also aided me in my endeavor.

In addition to Dr. Proctor's book, I was given beneficial information for this preaching project by Kelly Miller Smith in his book entitled *Social Crisis Preaching*, which was presented at the Lyman Beecher

Lectures in 1983. Smith sets the tone for preaching toward social activism in his proclamation:

> Social crises are precisely where the Christian minister should be found. The work of interpreting and rectifying wrongs in this area is the proper work of those who proclaim the Christian gospel. The words social crisis and preaching do belong together. As a matter of fact, the term preaching in the most profound meaning includes a concern with social crisis.[10]

Smith allows me to see that preaching must be concerned with rectifying the wrongs that occur in the community as well as among the people of God. Where there is a crisis, the preacher must be willing to address the issues that surround the crisis. Preaching must be more than just a message of living in glory. The one who stands and preaches must lift up his or her voice in order to deal with the social issues that are at hand.

Smith believes that preaching can be an important tool to address any situation in which one finds him- or herself. I believe that the voice God gives preachers can be used as a medium to share truths that will lead to change in those who are open to hear. As Smith suggests:

> When the social crisis-conscious preacher mounts the rostrum she or he has the responsibility of proclaiming the Word of God in all of its uncompromising power. It is a Word that speaks to the condition of the oppressed. It informs, it energizes, it convicts, it converts, and it blazes the trail for social changes. The Word of God is not static and placid; it is dynamic and unrelentingly disturbing.[11]

Preaching can move the people of God to be acclimated toward being socially active. Dr. Kelly Smith gives five points regarding a social crisis sermon:

- Social crisis sermons may be delivered with or without notes.
- Since social crisis preaching is done in times of heightened emotions and pronounced tensions, the preacher must strive to maintain control in sermon delivery while not removing nor diminishing the emotional element.
- The natural equipment of the preacher should determine the particular style of the delivery.
- Getting across a social crisis sermon will be aided by the employment of variety in pitch and force on the part of the preacher.
- Diaphragmatic breathing, clarity of enunciation, and projection of the voice will be most helpful in communicating a social crisis sermon.[12]

These five statements help social activist preachers by giving them practical help in the delivery of crisis sermons.

Perhaps the most important information I gained from Smith is that "the direct method may at times be chosen with the hope that the sheer forthrightness and honesty of the preacher will aid in getting reception for his or her crisis proclamation."[13] It is clear to me that when one preaches on social activism, he or she must speak clearly and make sure that the focus of the sermon is understood. The preacher must know what is being suggested through the sermon, and the people who hear the sermon must likewise know what the preacher is suggesting. Sometimes the preacher will find him- or herself dealing with some difficult issues, but he or she must also be willing to speak the truth boldly.

The point of speaking clearly on the crisis issue leads to the preaching of Harry Emerson Fosdick, who is considered to be the master of the art of persuasion in preaching. Fosdick's type of preaching—preaching with a purpose in mind—is what social activism is all about. In his famous essay "What Is the Matter with Preaching?" Fosdick writes:

> Every sermon should have for its main business the solving of some problem—a vital important problem, puzzling minds, burdening consciences, distracting lives... There is nothing that people are so interested in as themselves....That is basic. No preaching that neglects it can ripple a congregation....and until that ideal of it commands a preacher's mind and method, eloquence will avail him little and theology not at all.[14]

A sermon must have a purpose; the message must deal with this purpose. Preaching with a purpose looks at a problem and then offers a solution. Halford R. Ryan comments on Fosdick's problem solution in his book *Harry Emerson Fosdick: Persuasive Preacher*: "The problem solution pattern, wherein the orator states a problem and advocates a solution, aims at actuation."[15]

This is exactly what preaching on social activism does. It always raises problems and hopes to move those who hear the message toward a life of social activism. When one preaches with this aim in mind, those who hear the profound message are motivated.

I have concluded that those who preach on social activism must also deal with the emotional process of those who make up the congregation. Preaching is not merely presenting sermons; the one who preaches from behind the sacred desk must also deal with the emotional process of those who hear the sermon as it is preached. The author Dr. Frank Thomas declares that "western preaching has ignored the emotional context and process, and focused on the cerebral process and words, that homileticians most recently have struggled for new methods to effectively communicate the gospel."[16] The social activist preacher must not leave out the emotional process in his sermon preparation. Instead, he or she must let it be the key factor in sermon preparation.

In preaching to promote social activism, one will deal with many of the social ills that plague the congregation as well as address the problems of society at large. The congregation should not just be beaten over the head with a list of problems but should be able to celebrate that with God in the puzzle, there is hope for a change. It is important that preachers move toward a goal in their preaching. Dealing with the emotional in no way diminishes the total message; it is a part of the total message. The preaching context is as important as the rhetoric or words one uses in preaching, but in addition to this, one has to deal with the emotions.

Dr. Thomas suggests that dialectical preaching is like a piece of music that moves toward an ending. All of the pieces of the musical composition are important to the whole musical piece. Thomas says:

> Each movement in a piece of music expresses a certain nuance or shade of meaning that registers in the emotive. Each movement builds upon the emotive effect of the previous movement, heightening and enhancing the melody that has already been created, until at the close of the piece, one is left with a clear meaning or experience that registers in the intuitive.[17]

It is important that at the end, one is able to celebrate the good news that has been shared in the message. Many African American preachers use what is called "intonation" or "whooping" at the end of the message to close their sermon celebration. If one deals with emotion by "whooping," one must have specific contents before one uses intonation: "Intonation can be an appropriate and powerful vehicle for celebration when it is natural and authentic to the preacher and congregation, and when it reinforces the truth already taught."[18] One has to be cognizant that whooping must be done in connection with the power of the Holy Spirit.

The design of preaching toward social activism should include certain things that will give the sermon more direction and exclude things that can hamper the sermon quality and structure. Specifically, three things that should be excluded are as follows:

- The preacher is an expert at analyzing the problem (the bad news) but a novice at concrete gospel solutions that give people hope, and therefore the sermon has more bad news than good news;
- The lack of clarity, purpose, and focus takes listeners down side roads, and listeners notice they are miles off any course that the sermon might be traveling toward resolution;
- The purpose of the sermon is unclear, and therefore listeners miss what they are to do as a result of the sermon and how they are being invited to biblical change.[19]

In his book *A Guide to Preaching*, R. E. O. White challenges preachers to employ the power of the sermon to persuade congregants to react to social crises. This view coincides with the sentiments presented by Fosdick about preaching toward a purpose. Trying to lead the congregation toward social activism is a form of persuasion. The pastor preaches to persuade the parish or people to a level of involvement. White explains,

> The purpose of the preacher has to be communicated to the congregation, to become their purpose also. Something has to be kindled, moved, and achieved, while the service proceeds. The truth must be shared, not merely passed from one mind to other minds in words, but so that it comes to belong to both, and grips both speaker and hearers. Preaching is from faith to faith—from the conviction of the preacher, to convincing of the listener before God.[20]

Using persuasion, the preacher urges people toward the truth. Persuasion is not to be used in order to deceive the people into some action of wrongdoing, and it is not used to deceive people in order to satisfy the preacher's wants. It should not be used to move people to do something that is not the will of God.

I believe that the persuasion has to be done according to the Word of God. Persuasion toward social activism has its roots and theology in the Word of God. Social activism is persuading people to live and follow the Word of God. The object for the social activist preacher is to move the people to the understanding that God is calling on them to be instruments of social activism. The social activist preacher should preach to solicit an active response from those who hear the message. This means that the pastor must know his congregation. White says, "A sensitive preacher is aware of, and responsive to, the traditions, the prejudices, the level of culture, the commanding interest and problems of every audience."[21]

According to Henry H. Mitchell in his book *Recovery of Preaching*, a pastor can know his flock by sitting where they sit: "The recovery of preaching in America is heavily dependent on the willingness and ability of preachers to sit where the people sit, existentially and culturally."[22] This statement of sitting where the people sit is important for the preacher who is preaching toward social activism because in order to lead the people to do something, the preacher must know where they are intellectually, socially, and spiritually. When one prepares a social activist sermon, he or she must keep in mind who will hear it.

It is imperative that those who hear the message can relate to what the preacher is saying. The preacher must present the message using content and delivery that are generally understandable to the congregation and relative to their existence. This means that the preacher must keep in mind that many people who make up the congregation may not be "at the same place," yet the preacher must attempt to reach them where they are. All attempts to move people to be socially active involve communicating to them on their level. The ability to communicate with his or her audience allows the preacher to reach those who hear the message. Only when the preacher reaches them can he or she move them.

Along with Dr. Frank Thomas, Dr. Mitchell also informs about behavior in social activist preaching. Mitchell talks about a behavioral purpose, which was important toward developing this model. Every sermon that leads toward social activism must have a behavioral purpose. Mitchell states,

> Every sermon will have a controlling ideal and require some intellectual growth or an increased understanding, but maturity of attitude and behavior—deep trust, with willing obedience—is the central objective. The purpose should embody the action demanded by the biblical text, and should reflect the preacher's gut motivation for writing the sermon, even though the main ideal may be negative. The challenge is to convert a negative motivating ideal to a positive behavioral purpose that flows out of the text.[23]

This behavioral purpose helped me stay focused in my preaching toward social activism. Preaching toward social activism requires the preacher to deal with many negative statements. In fact, the preacher may have to raise many negative issues to move listeners to positive action. Social injustices, disparities, and other social ills that are in the world may inevitably surface. The purpose must be a part of the life—or as Mitchell suggests, the gut—of the preacher. In addition to this negative aspect, the preacher must also use the purpose of behavioral statement to move toward something that is positive. This change in the behavior of people is positive. With this in mind, there is action in preaching for this study, and the action, or behavioral change, is toward social activism.

As a change agent, the pastor in the African American pulpit has power. Pastors moving people toward action have the power of the pulpit behind them. Wyatt T. Walker, a strong advocate of the power of the pulpit, says, "The black preacher fires the hopes and aspirations of the oppressed community and became in turn, a symbolic medicine man for all the ills that occur."[24] For Wyatt, the preacher is of "inestimable" value. I believe that the voice of the pastor who stands behind the sacred desk in the black community has the power to lead the people of God toward a change. Many who stand behind the pulpit have the power but do not use it effectively to manifest a change in the minds, hearts, or lives of the people by moving them toward social activism.

In Gardner C. Taylor's book *How Shall They Preach*, he states, "It is this kind of gnawing uncertainty about the value and worth of preaching which will doubtless afflict all of us from time to time. For one, I confess that preaching has often seemed to be such a clumsy and unclear form of communication."[25] I am in disagreement with this statement. I do not doubt the power of preaching. When preaching is done utilizing the right method and motive, it is always a powerful means of communication. My belief, drawn from my own convictions and observations, is one that has seen and still believes in the power of the preached word.

Taylor, in *How Shall They Preach*, gave me a clearer understanding relative to how the preacher's own experiences affect his power and presentation of the Word of God. Dr. Taylor states,

> The power and pathos of the preacher are to be found not in volume of voice nor those patently contrived tremors of tone preachers sometimes affect, but in passionate avowals which are passionate because they have gotten out of the written word into the preacher's own heart, have been filtered and colored by the preacher's own experiences of joy and sorrow, and then are presented to and pressed upon the heart and minds of those who hear.[26]

This helps me to realize that in social crisis preaching, the words that one speaks must be a part of his or her life. It is important that the social crisis message is a part of the preacher's life. If the preacher does not believe it, how can he or she expect those who hear the message to be touched or moved toward social activism? We often hear the expression, "What comes from the heart reaches the heart." I am acutely cognizant that to reach people, one must rely on the Holy Spirit.

As one who values the power of the Holy Spirit, I realize its importance in this project. Three authors brought this to a clearer understanding for me: Evans E. Crawford, Henry Mitchell, and James Forbes. It was Crawford who emphasized that there must be "the interrelationship of the Holy Spirit, the preacher, and the congregation and the nature of the transaction that takes place among them as the word of God is proclaimed."[27] It is my belief that it takes more than just speaking powerful words from the Bible or delivering wonderfully structured messages to move the people. It takes the presence of God in the framework of the congregation, in the pastor and in the people. For Crawford, the word must be spoken, and the people must see and hear, and this must happen in conjunction with the Spirit. The Holy Spirit, manifesting Himself, can cause the believer to act upon what is heard and react to what is felt. For me, the Spirit in preaching does more than excite. He also causes one to move on what has been heard.

Preaching toward social activism takes more than just the power of the preacher; it takes the power of the Holy Spirit. The pastor or preacher must not stand in self but in the power of God. In his book *The Holy Spirit & Preaching*, James Forbes states, "There are many who are aware that if that power is not present, the preaching will not be effective."[28] For preaching to be effective, it must incorporate the Spirit of God. Mitchell agrees with this truth: "The preacher is only an instrument in the hands of God, who saves all the souls who are saved, and who stimulates living faith using catalysts called preachers, who are guided by the holy spirit."[29] It is this Spirit that can move the preacher to be a catalyst and an instrument for social activism.

In addition to presenting valuable insights regarding preaching, Forest Harris, in *Ministry for Social Crisis*, instilled in me a deep realization that there are congregations who have taken on the role of social activist. He presented examples of different models for ministry that can be effective for communities in crisis. This enabled me to see that with different situations, there are various manners of ministry that can make a difference.

In Harris's book, he lists five different congregations who have taken on the spirit of social activism and touched the lives of many people. Harris states, "...nor are they presented as models which must be duplicated in all congregations and communities."[30] I realize that I may not have the ability to duplicate these different ministries where I serve because God calls different churches to different ministries. God calls different pastors and people to different ministries for His kingdom. Harris, however, gives a picture of what the church can do by being socially active. The ministries he presents helped me form a model of the types of creative things that I can do where I serve.

In addition to Forest Harris, another author, Grant S. Shockley, was very helpful with the model of social activism. Shockley's article "Black Pastoral Leadership in Religious Education: Social Crisis Correlates" deals with the fact that few churches have social programs. I argue against this point because I see that many of my affiliate churches have some social action ministries in place. I have a problem with blanket statements such as "Most churches and pastors are not involved in social actions" and "If they are just giving money, no matter how minute, they are making a contribution."

Shockley does, however, present helpful information on the mission of the church. He states that the church mission deals with social activism. Shockley discusses social justice, objectives, educational strategies, models, and the leadership component from the black religious experience. He allows me to see that as a pastor, I play a key role in leading my people to become socially active. According to Shockley,

> Pastors have an exciting opportunity to model and stimulate others to become engaged in social justice ministries. It is clear that the pastor is the key person in this development of a vision and strategy for the education of members of the faith community concerning the genuine problems and issues facing our society.[31]

This reinforces the power the pastor has from the pulpit in leading a congregation to become socially active. Shockley's article gave me a keen awareness that the work of the pastor is of utmost importance in social activism.

The sources that I have presented in this chapter are all essential to the development and implementation of this project. They serve as a catalyst and means of inspiration, hope, and understanding to bring meaning to preaching that produces the norm of social activism. These different works make up the literature review for this project.

Chapter 2 Notes

_____
_____
_____
_____
_____
_____
_____
_____
_____
_____
_____
_____
_____
_____
_____
_____
_____
_____
_____
_____
_____
_____

Theological Foundation of Preaching That Leads to Social Activism

The process of calling the people of God into an awareness of God's saving, liberating and redemptive acts so as to compel the radical participation of individuals and communities in spiritual, social and personal transformation. The result of that transformation will be the realization of human wholeness and potential in the present as well as the future.[32] — **Carlyle Fielding Stewart**

Statement of Focus

Preaching has always been considered to be a very important part of the mission, ministry, and mandate of the church. Having preached the gospel of Jesus Christ nearly all of my life, I believe that the church can reclaim power over the congregation through the preaching of the gospel. The Word of God should be the central focus of a worship experience and the primary means of motivating God's people to act. I agree with Carlyle Fielding Stewart's position that there is power in the preached Word of God that can transform the lives of people who take heed. In the preached Word, there is power to change hearts, minds, talk, and behavior.

My focus is that preaching the gospel in an African American context can bring about social change. My emphasis is on biblical preaching in the African American tradition that establishes the norm for social activism. Social passivism is the problem in ministry at St. Paul, which is my context.

Looking seriously at St. Paul, one will find that most people in our congregation are not socially active in our surrounding community because they fear the repercussions of moving from maintenance to ministry. They simply want to conform rather than to transform. They feel that social activism is the exception rather than the general rule in the church.

Conversely, I debate the issue that social activism is the exception rather than the norm in the Christian environment, the majority community, and the black community. I am cognizant of the fact that people in the church quickly vocalize the existing problems yet slowly supply solutions. They fail to put solutions into action. Problems in the church and community are clearly visible, yet church people in their comfort zones fail to get involved in solving them. In the black society, too often we look for help from others outside our communities instead of seeking help from those within our own communities. We must somehow become socially active in our own communities if we are going to progress and make this world a better place for all people to live.

In my opinion, at the St. Paul Church (where I serve as pastor), we are aware of many social problems, but we have yet to move toward providing solutions to these problems. The objective of my project is to develop a series of eight sermons that will motivate the members of St. Paul to become socially active.

By social activism, I mean that the church will work to make things better. Social activism means being a part of a movement that wants to work and help improve the well-being of society. More specifically, social activism means working to make things better for the poor, sick, handicapped, oppressed, disenfranchised, hurt, hopeless, and enslaved. In this book, I will demonstrate or illustrate how biblical preaching can encourage people to become socially active.

When we take a serious look at the Word of God, we can see "operation social activism theology" in practice. The idea of being socially active is rooted in the Word of God. The pastor of a church must take charge under the Holy Spirit and lead the people into carrying out Christ's mission. Part of this mission includes preaching and teaching social activism. Preaching social activism is the "balm in Gilead" that will make the poor, sick, handicapped, disenfranchised, hurt, hopeless, and enslaved whole.

A series of successfully transmitted social activism sermons is the key that will lock the door to social passivism and unlock the door to social activism. Preaching was the source of social activism in the past;

likewise, preaching is our source today. I wholeheartedly agree with Dr. Samuel D. Proctor, who says, "Today's preachers are required to define, to declare and defend the gospel in the twentieth and twenty-first centuries with the same relevance, zeal, and commitment that Paul, Ambrose, Augustine, Aquinas, Luther, and Richard Allen brought to their times."[33]

Theological Foundations

When I consider the theological foundation for social activism, three key questions come to mind: Where is God in all of this? What does God have to say about preaching in terms of social activism? How does the Word of God give substance to preaching that eventually leads to social activism? I believe the answers to these questions can form or build a solid theological foundation.

First, I want to talk about the nature of preaching. Secondly, I will look at the Old Testament, which illustrates God's practice of social activism through the prophets. Thirdly, I will look at the New Testament ministry of Jesus, who was a social activist. Finally, I will look at the messages of other preachers who have influenced my understanding of social activism and have helped me build this faith in the believers' hearts and minds at St. Paul.

What Is Preaching?

First, one must understand what preaching means. According to Fred B. Craddock, "Preaching is the concerted engagement of one's faculties of body, mind and spirit. It is then a skilled activity. Preaching has to do with a particular content and a certain message converged."[34] The message a preacher delivers is not comprised of a few random words but, rather, words spoken to lead people to a better way of life. Preaching not only tells us about how people were helped in the past but also speaks to the present. Preaching addresses the many hurdles and obstacles that people must endure. I agree with the position of Olin P. Moyd:

> And, in spite of all the social, political, and economic obstacles challenging the existence and progress of this people, preaching has been the primary vehicle for transmitting transcendent theological truths to the homes and the hearts of the masses. Educational centers and programs are in operation by African American churches and institutions across this nation, but I contend that even with these centers and these programs, which were not so prevalent (in the past), still the majority of the religionists in these communities get their theology from the preached Word rather than through the various Christian educational ministries.[35]

Preaching should persuade people to make a difference in their churches and communities. The preachers' sermons should lead congregations to establish programs that will meet the needs of the poor, sick, handicapped, disenfranchised, hurt, hopeless, and enslaved.

Paul describes the role of the preacher in Romans 10:14-15:

> *How then shall they call on him in whom they have not believed? And how shall they believe in him of whom they have not heard? And how shall they hear without a preacher? And how shall they preach, except they be sent? As it is written, how beautiful are the feet of them that preach the gospel of peace, and bring glad tidings of good things!* — ***Romans 10:14-15 (KJV)***

When the congregation hears the Word from the preacher, they are encouraged to go in the name of the Lord and do what needs to be done. Paul illustrates how people can hear because they allow themselves to hear the preacher who is sent by God. The God-sent preacher brings tidings of good things from God. As God's representative, the preacher has the tremendous task of motivating the congregation to become socially active. The good news of the gospel is the holistic approach to salvation. Jesus saves the whole man. He meets physical as well as spiritual needs.

Preaching Technique

Preaching intended to lead people to become socially active must be done by a particular method. The method that I used is known as the dialectical method. This method stems from the German philosopher Georg Wilhelm Friedrich Hegel.

This is a form based on the so-called in some quarters the Hegelian scheme. It is based upon the philosophy of George Wilhelm Friedrich Hegel who developed a notion of the conflict of opposites that could be resolved only with the recognition of their interdependence. Contradictory realities imply and require each other, according to this perspective as evident in Hegel's Philosophy and History and his Philosophy of Right, which include the thesis, the antithesis, and the synthesis.[36]

I was introduced to this method through my readings from Samuel Proctor and Kelly Smith. Each of these preachers and authors speaks of this method as being helpful and beneficial for motivational preaching. This method of preaching gives reality to the concept of the gospel being used to convert people to social activism. This method allows people to view their problems through the lens of Scripture and offers solutions helpful in dealing with the problems. It allows the preacher to discuss the ills a pastor and people are facing in order to bring hope in the midst of trials and difficult situations. This dialectical method also allows a preacher to discuss issues and change the minds and hearts of some people enough to influence them to make a difference. In addition to the dialectical method, I have used some other ideas from preachers to enhance my style of preaching.

God

When I view the Old Testament, I clearly see that God is a social activist. This theology stems from history, in which God has always been active. To think of God's social activism is to think of His creation of earth and man. Being active rather than passive, God is responsible for the world, water, land, sky, and people. The lives that God made in the past as well as the present illustrate His activity.

God was also active by making His presence known and by participating in the lives of man. Looking at the Bible, one can see that God was active in giving His chosen people laws to govern and make their society more just. God was concerned about how they treated one another daily in communal life. God was concerned about social justice. God wanted the lives of His children to be examples for the world. He wanted other nations to see that He was God and His children's lives were representative of Him. God's social activism is illustrated to us through messengers in the Bible. These messengers whom God used as instruments of social activism were called prophets.

God gave His prophets certain messages that moved the people from social passivism to social activism. These prophets were more concerned about correcting social injustice than they were about gaining popularity. Walter Brueggeman says, "It is the vocation of the prophet to keep alive the ministry of imagination, to keep on conjuring and proposing alternative futures to the single one the king wants to urge as the only thinkable one."[37] The prophets did not accept the status quo but spoke out to those who were in power to make changes occur in social injustice. The prophets did not disillusion the people about the negative things going wrong in the world around them. Instead, they confronted the people of God about all of their shortcomings and led them to a better way of life.

Many preachers today leave the call to social activism out of their messages. In fact, many successful preachers appear to be satisfied with maintaining social passivism. To include the idea of social activism in preaching challenges the preacher to know him- or herself as well as those to whom he ministers. Preaching that brings about social activism must be flavored with demographics. According to Walter Brueggemann, "This new importance, which attaches to the contemporary preaching, is an importance of depth and not one to be interpreted in terms of a widespread attraction to preaching made popular and palatable with mild heat of holy oratory."[38] Like the prophets of old, contemporary preachers must tailor their messages of social activism to meet the needs of specific congregations.

Often when we look at the Scriptures, we tend to view them only as events that happened in the past. Some people would even argue that the Scriptures have no relevance to the present. However, when I study the prophets of the Old Testament, I learn that they spoke out in times of crisis. They spoke on behalf of the Lord against the injustices of the land. They spoke against how the rich mistreated the poor. They realized how their present situations in the world were not consistent with what God proclaimed as righteousness. They became conscious of the widespread unholiness that occurred in the framework of daily temple life. They realized how people were transacting business in their fraudulent markets.

Today's preachers must follow the pattern of the prophets. According to Samuel Proctor, "As pastors, we are called to be involved in the lives of people. We are among the first to feel the pain of violent oppression, unmitigated suffering and long term neglect as they erupt in episodic crises in their various communities."[39] The prophets were cognizant of the unjust situations that existed within their various communities, and they were willing to become socially active. Through preaching, God's spokesperson must develop messages that accentuate the positives of social activism rather than the negatives of social activism that help to promote social injustice.

Message of the Prophets

As we look at the social injustice in the world today, we see that most people are in need of prophetic preaching to speak to their hearts and urge them to positive action. Our world is certainly in a terrible condition. In a larger sense, we are living in perilous times. Prophetic preaching "aims at setting corrective measures into motion. Social crisis preaching is calculated to yield a practical good with regard to the most painful problems of society."[40]

Social activism is both implicit and explicit in the messages of the prophets. One of the prophets who comes to mind when thinking of social activism is Amos. This man of God was not rich by any scope of the imagination. Amos lived in Tekoa, a bleak district of Palestine. He picked sycamore fruit, food that was eaten by the poorest people. He could have stayed home in his comfort zone, where he was working and living with his family, but he was willing to leave and go to the northern kingdom to become socially active.

Amos left home with a message against the false religious idol worshippers and the oppressors of the poor. He preached and proclaimed a message to lead his people to responsibility and commitment to God. He boldly spoke out the words of God to oppressors "because they sold the righteous for silver, and the poor for a pair of shoes; that pant after the dust of the earth on the head of the poor, and turn aside the way of the meek" (Amos 2:6-7 KJV).

In his socially active role, Amos openly voiced how the poor of his time were mistreated. The people of his day had been committing social injustice so long that they felt their actions were right. Amos says, "For they know not to do right" (Amos 3:10 KJV). Their wrongdoing blinded them from the truth. Amos, however, helped them take their blinders off and see that God forbade their gross injustices.

Likewise, preachers today must help society to remove the blinders and see social injustice. God does not want us to be naïve about or blind to wrongdoing. Just as He used Amos to speak for Him in Bible days, He still uses preachers to be His spokespersons today. God does not make people robots or puppets; we are free to make our own choices. When we make the wrong choice, however, God steps in to correct us. In the midst of injustice and sin, God calls us back to repentance through the preachers. If we don't take heed, He will judge our actions in the end.

God's word for social activism in Amos's day was "let justice run down like water, and righteousness like a mighty stream" (Amos 5:24 NKJV). When I reflect upon the injustices of Amos's day, I realize that the people were merely going through the motion of religion, but they did not exemplify righteousness. Like modern-day Christians, they were religious, but they were not regenerated in their hearts.

Like Amos, contemporary preachers of the gospel must speak out against injustice, racism, failures of society, and any other ills within it. This is what I conclude from studying the messages of God's prophets. We should become active just like Amos did. I strongly agree with Samuel Proctor that

> Someone must stand on the wall and cry Woe! However, along with social activism and prophetic words, people should be educated about religious matters to have comfort in life's crises. They need an impetus to serve, participate, and create alliances to address the issues so glaring in the pastor's sermon.[41]

As illustrated through the prophet Amos, God's Word has power to make His people socially active.

Ministry of Jesus

The message of the prophets or the message of social activism is also seen in the life of Jesus. Jesus reiterated the words of the prophet Isaiah when He spoke out concerning the method of His ministry:

> *The Spirit of the Lord is upon me, because he hath anointed me to preach the gospel to the poor; he hath sent me to heal the brokenhearted, to preach deliverance to the captives, and recovering of sight to the blind, to set at liberty them that are bruised, to preach the acceptable year of the Lord.* — *Luke 4:18-19 (KJV)*

This passage of Scripture embodies the whole life of Jesus Christ. I believe this is the message that shows that Jesus was the leader in the issue of social activism. My philosophy of Jesus is that He was socially active because He fought against a totally unjust system and society. Christ, the greatest preacher of all time, was a social activist. He spoke against the religious system that somehow forgot God's purpose for the people to make a difference in society. Jesus was willing to be socially active for the poor, sick, prison-bound, blind, and downtrodden. I believe the people of God should follow the example of Jesus Christ.

In reviewing the words of Christ, I am reminded that He believed in being socially active in the service of God.

*For I was an hungred, and ye gave me meat: I was thirsty, and ye gave me drink: I was a stranger, and ye took me in: Naked, and ye clothed me: I was sick, and ye visited me: I was in prison, and ye came unto me. — **Matthew 25:35-36 (KJV)***

This passage of Scripture shows how God wants us not only to pray but also to take an active role in helping the less fortunate. We who are a part of the body of Christ are His representatives in the world to those in need. In Jesus' day, the less fortunate were often overlooked, but Jesus effectively ministered to their needs.

Like Jesus, the people of God today should be concerned about feeding the hungry, clothing the naked, housing the homeless, and visiting the sick and imprisoned. Simply stated, I feel that the life of Jesus was socially active because He met with people and wholeheartedly ministered to them. When God blesses a congregation with resources, they should actively be involved in ministry that will truly allow them to be help for the helpless and hope for the hopeless in the community.

Jesus Christ was the greatest preacher of all time because He spoke out energetically, boldly, and emphatically for desperate and deprived individuals. Moreover, Samuel Proctor reminds us:

Through the proclamation of the prophets, through history and poetry, Judaism addresses social concerns. From its inception, Christianity has concerned itself with social problems. The coming of Jesus and his words and ministry had profound social and political meaning.[42]

It is crystal clear that as a social activist, Jesus did not conform to the status quo that promoted social injustice. Jesus was a social worker who transformed the lives of the poor, sick, handicapped, disenfranchised, hurt, hopeless, and enslaved. Preachers today must become social workers who motivate their congregation to social activism. Jesus is our best example; the hallmark of His message is social activism or helping others.

People

Finally, I want to focus on the message of other individuals who have influenced me to believe in the practice of social activism. As I reflect upon the history of the African American race here in the United States, I see that many individuals were instrumental in giving me this model of social activism. First of all, I think of the slaves who lived in this country in bondage. A few social activists appear from my African American history. I think of historical figures like Denmark Vesey, who planned a revolt against the system of slavery in Charleston, South Carolina. His plan was never executed because he was hanged. I also think of individuals like Frederick A. Douglass, spoke out against slavery, risking his own life because he was against the evils of slavery.

Leaders such as William Edward Burghart DuBois, one of the founders of the NAACP, have certainly had an impact on my vision for leading God's people toward social activism. Russell L. Adams says of DuBois, "Throughout his life he hacked at the enslaving chains of racism and prejudice with the sword of scientific truth, and thrust the flame of intellect into the dark caves of degrading myth and stereotype."[43] It is this historical perspective, along with many others, that have given birth to my theology for social activism. These black historical figures could have settled for selfish, passive lifestyles, but they were willing to work in order to make a difference.

Pastors and Churches

I have witnessed black pastors who are free from confinement to a pulpit inside the stained-glass windows of a church. One such pastor was my father, Dr. J. J. Taylor, Sr. I believe that his life as a pastor and preacher touched me to become involved in social change. He was concerned about more than preaching on Sunday morning. He believed in a ministry that affected lives. He was also concerned about helping children through day care, helping seniors through housing projects, and teaching trades to individuals that needed to be rehabilitated and made honest citizens in society.

My father reared me to be concerned about the plight of other human beings. His entire life was one of social activism. He was always trying to minister to the total person. He opened a day-care center to help develop a solid religious foundation for young children. He was able to build a sixty-unit apartment building for decent housing for people on fixed incomes. He began a construction company and hired laborers who could not obtain jobs with other companies. Thus, he enabled pastors to build churches and helped the unemployed. As I reflect upon my father's life, I am compelled to a socially active ministry.

In addition to my father, Vernon Johns influenced me. He was a minister who was not afraid to speak the truth about the injustice of the white community. Other ministers like Dr. Wyatt T. Walker and Dr. Martin Luther King, Jr., who became martyrs for social justice, are also my inspiration for social activism. These brave preachers have encouraged me to be God's instrument to bring about social change and correct the ills of society through preaching the Word.

I believe God always sends forth prophets to deal with different social crises in the community. In times of crisis, God appoints and anoints a man or woman. As I read the Old Testament, I discovered that where there was a need, God always appointed a spokesman. God still appoints spokespersons such as Dr. Martin Luther King, Jr., who was willing to venture from his pulpit and the four walls of the church to minister in the streets.

It was King who inspired ministers of all faiths and ethnic backgrounds to understand that there are times when marching in the streets and protesting injustice in whatever arena are continuous with, not separate from or contradictory to, the pulpit ministry.[44] — **Kelly Smith**

Some ministers today who were motivated by King are still active in the fight for African American people.

One of these prominent leaders of today is the Baptist minister Rev. Jesse Jackson. He is still active in working for Black Americans through Operation PUSH and the Rainbow Coalition. The black preachers that I have mentioned are the leaders who come to mind when I think of people who engaged in social activism.

Presently, there are a few churches that model social activism in the Chicago area. One of these models is the Antioch Missionary Baptist Church, pastored by Dr. W. N. Daniel. This pastor has given his life to speaking out against social ills, and he has worked to make a difference in the community. He has been successful in the Englewood area, where the church is providing low-income housing and senior-citizen homes.

His ministry shows me how a powerful preacher can use the pulpit to lead his people to make a difference in the community. As a beacon light, this particular church has transformed many blocks in the community. Dr. Daniel believes that "the church has to be concerned about the total man, and his own preaching gives people confidence to follow him. The church must not only be concerned about getting people to heaven but also giving them some comfort on earth."[45]

Another church that models social activism in the Chicago area is the Emmanuel Baptist Church of Chicago, pastored by Dr. L. K. Curry. This church is especially important to me because it has one of the leading black Christian grammar schools in this country. The number of young black children that are taught in this Christian environment by the church ministry inspires me to use this church as a model. I believe this model of education is one that black churches all over the country can appreciate and follow. Emmanuel Baptist is also providing jobs for Christian adults who are teaching a new generation of children to follow in Christ's footsteps.

My mentor, Dr. George MacRae, Pastor of the Mt. Tabor Baptist Church, Miami, Florida, also has a church that models social activism. His church has a feeding program for the poverty-stricken community of Liberty City. In addition, the church has an AIDS ministry that has not abandoned those who are the least, the lowly, and the left out. His drug program deals with the problem of drug users and helps families that are trying to come to grips with the problem of drug addiction. This church has a prison ministry for inmates while they are incarcerated and when they are released from the prison system. The church is also actively involved in the broken or strained relationships in families that have been torn apart because of a spouse's incarceration.

Many churches all over the country have embraced a holistic approach to ministry. There are also ministries throughout the country that have followed their pastors from the pulpit to social activism. Leroy Fitts reports:

> Such areas as medical care, recreation, housing, counseling, problems of the aging, youth centers, business enterprises, food co-ops, credit unions, and other social ministries have found central positions in the scope of ministry among Black Baptists. To be sure, Black Baptists have concretized the social gospel rhetoric of the Christian church.[46]

I wholeheartedly believe that the preaching of the gospel can lead to social activism. I have shown how some prophets practiced this method through preaching. I have also viewed the ministry of Jesus and explained how He was a socially active preacher. Finally, I discussed how some preachers have inspired me and strengthened my belief that God wants us to be socially active. Motivated by the prophets of old, Jesus, historians, and contemporary preachers, I hereby accept the challenge to lead the members of the St. Paul congregation to embrace a socially active ministry.

Chapter 3 Notes

Operation Restoration: Eight Sermons That Inspire Social Change

Sermon 1: Hope in the Midst of Hopelessness (Ezekiel 37:1-9)

Please look with me today at a very familiar and well-known passage of Scripture from the Word of God. This passage of Scripture has been preached, taught, and shared by many preachers and believers on several occasions. Every time I read, study, and meditate on this passage, I find myself receiving new thoughts, hopes, and aspirations. This passage is centered on a prophet of God named Ezekiel, who had many strange and unusual visions. Many have viewed this prophet of God as strange and unusual. Some have suggested that he was paranoid, schizophrenic, psychotic, or crazy, but God gave him strange visions to share a spiritual truth. One of the strange and unusual visions Ezekiel had is the subject of our message today, "Hope in the Midst of Hopelessness." It is the vision of dry bones in the valley found in Ezekiel 37:1-9.

This passage of Scripture was written at a time when it seemed that all hope was gone. It was a period in the lives of God's children in which they felt that there was no hope ahead. Some people would argue today that we are living in the midst of hopelessness. For example, one may look at our church and community and say that there is no hope. One may look at our children and say there is no hope. One may contend that it will get worse before it gets better. But the focal point of my message today is that there is hope in the midst of hopelessness.

In Ezekiel's vision of dry bones, I clearly perceive that when God is in the picture, dry bones can live again. I believe the God that I serve can truly bring hope in the mist of hopelessness. Therefore, I challenge us to look at this passage of Scripture and find hope in the midst of our hopelessness. Let us review the vision from this eccentric prophet, Ezekiel, and witness how God used him to communicate the age-old spiritual truth that God can bring hope when it seems that all hope is gone.

Problem of Hope

The city of Jerusalem had been ransacked, and the temple had been destroyed. The symbolic vision expressed in verse 11 indicates that "the whole house of Israel" was in the midst of hopelessness (Ezekiel 37:11 KJV). Israel was a nation that had been defeated in its military conquest. The people had become exiles, and they believed that God had walked away and left them. These people, and the community in general, were low in spirit; they felt all their hope was gone: "Alone, exhausted, discouraged, and impoverished, Israel was as good as dead."[47] The hopelessness of exile seemed so overwhelming to them that they literally hung their heads in despair.

Listen to what verse 11 proclaims: "Our bones are dried, and our hope is lost: we are cut off for our parts" (Ezekiel 37:11 KJV). They had no hope. I believe hope means to expect fully, and hopeless means not to expect fully. In addition, to be hopeless means to be despairing, desperate, downhearted, disconsolate, and downtrodden. To be hopeless means to feel that the sun will not shine again and the mountains will get higher while the valleys get lower.

When I think about the situation of the Israelites in the text, I think of my own situation as a pastor with a congregation. Being of African descent, surely we can understand what it means to be hopeless. The Englewood community, in which our church is located, used to be considered important because it offered excellent suburban transportation. According to the *Local Community Fact Book*,

The unemployment rate in Englewood is more than 18 percent. The number of housing units had dropped from 28,000 to 19,000 in the last three decades, and one in eight residents live in overcrowded conditions. The dependency rate is high; 40 percent is less than 18 years old and female's head more than half the households with children under 18. The median family income is among the lowest in the city and more than a third of all residents live in poverty.[48]

This community has some residents who are living in sad, depressing situations, and there appears to be no hope for them. The average household income in 1989 was a minute $13,243, which is below the average means of survival. Many people who live "on the doorsteps of our church" are maintaining lives that will lead to destruction because drugs are killing them, alcohol is destroying them, and people with gutter mentalities are killing them. This community is dying because of dilapidated housing, black-on-black crime, and homes that have become a battleground of hate, violence, abuse, low morals, and unholiness.

As I look at the degradation our young people in this community face today, I see what appears to be a hopeless situation. For example, our children are trapped in a system that poorly educates them. They attend school, receive bad grades, and graduate, but they are predominantly illiterate. They don't receive the type of family support needed to equip them with decent moral standards in their life. Being made sacrificial lambs, they are forced to live in an environment that discreetly encourages them to be complete failures. With poor education and poor home training, they emerge into adulthood with inadequate job skills and unhealthful personality traits.

Meanwhile, the church is going through the motions of religion and doing nothing to show they are part of the active body of Christ. The church has forgotten its call to discipleship, which is to make the world a better place. The church must embrace the evangelism movement which seeks to help the poor, sick, handicapped, oppressed, disenfranchised, hurt, hopeless, and enslaved.

Powerful Question of Hope

Today's text raises a question of hope. The Lord asks the prophet Ezekiel a very significant question about hope in verse 3: "can these bones live?" (Ezekiel 37:3 KJV). What a question to ask a prophet of God in the midst of a valley that is full of dead, dry bones! Ezekiel, "can these bones live?" This question emphasized Judah's utter hopelessness. The Lord demanded to know from Ezekiel if there was any hope for the bones lying in the valley.

It would have been easy for this prophet to look at the situation and give an answer. In all honesty, had I been in Ezekiel's situation, I would have answered the question with a resounding "no." Who in their right mind would say that dead, dry bones could live again?

I believe there are many Christians in St. Paul who have answered this question negatively. When we view our circumstances and environment, we feel that our future has reached a dead end. We look at the Englewood community and think perhaps we should move our church to the suburbs, away from crime, or find a piece of prime real estate close to the expressway and build a phenomenal church. We continue to think there is no hope here on this corner because "they will break into our cars, break out our windows, and continue to sell drugs in front of the church."

Some of us contend that there is no hope for the children because they do not care. Their parents don't care. Their teachers don't care. They are locked into this unfavorable environment, locked out of anything positive, and left out in the end. It makes little sense to invest time, energy, and effort into helping young people.

In essence, however, these negative statements leave God out of the picture, deleting Him as a means to an end. The prophet Ezekiel's "no" would have revealed his disbelief in God, yet many of us today are answering "no." This only confirms our lack of faith when we are faced with a situation that causes us to feel hopeless. The "no" answer is typically from a human point of view and not a divine point of view.

From another perspective, one may find it presumptuous for the prophet to answer "yes" because of his ignorance of the intention of God. Ezekiel was not selfish but desired to do the will of God. The safest answer that he could offer was: "O Lord GOD, thou knowest" (Ezekiel 37:3 KJV). He told God, "These bones can live if You want them to." Ezekiel believed that God was in charge of the future and whatever God commanded to happen would happen. If God wanted the bones to live, they would live.

Proclamation of Hope

How will God bring life into the dry bones? How can God bring life into this church, this community, and these children? Thank God for His two-part formula, remedy, and prescription for the dry bones in the valley. The two-part formula for life presented in the text consists of preaching and the Holy Spirit. I believe preaching the gospel and the Spirit of God can make a difference. The Lord told Ezekiel to prophesy to the dry bones (Ezekiel 37:4); in Hebrew, prophesy means to preach.

I am a firm believer that God's Word can bring new life. There is power in the folly of preaching. Ezekiel preached, and there was action in the valley. Nevertheless, Ezekiel's preaching had to be intensified with the Holy Spirit in order to bring life into the bones. The Spirit of God must be residing in the bones for life to exist.

In the midst of hopelessness, God can generate life. There is no church so dead that God cannot bring new life. There is no community so low that God cannot lift it. There is no child so forsaken that God cannot embrace it and hold it in the highest regard. Operation restoration is possible because with God, all things are possible. Whenever and wherever God is involved, there is hope because God can create hope in the midst of hopelessness.

Sermon 2: Camouflaged Religion
(Amos 5:21-27)

Today we will look at the prophecy of Amos from the Old Testament. Amos was a godly man who gathered sycamore fruit; he was not rich by any scope of the imagination. Amos was a socially active prophet of God. He lived in Tekoa, a bleak district of Palestine. He picked food from the sycamore tree and herded sheep. Amos could have stayed home and worked, living with his family in the southern kingdom, but he was willing to travel to the northern kingdom to become socially active. From the text today, I want to draw an analogy between the life and times of Amos and the life and times of St. Paul.

In our text, Amos lived in a day and time when the people had what I would like to call camouflaged religion. Many Christians today live as though their religion were hidden "under a bushel" or within the walls of the church. I often wonder why people waste so much time stopping by the church without God, the church, the pastor, or righteousness on their minds. Is church membership something they just want on their resumes? Something to tell their parents? Or just something to share with their friends?

Many believers attend church regularly, yet their lives show only activity. So many people have nothing but an empty, camouflaged religion. Their religion appears to be "tell" rather than "show and tell." Their religion seems to be for their own benefit rather than for the benefit of God. I believe the people of God must have a religion with more than mere activity. They must have a religion of action. I believe God wants His churches to exhibit a religion of action. I believe God wants His churches to exhibit a religion that flows in and out of the sanctuary.

I want to review this text about Amos today to emphasize that the social injustice that was prevalent in Amos's day is still prevalent in our society today. Moreover, like many of God's people in Amos's day, many of us are "social passivists." We need to become social activists like Amos.

Worship as an Activity

As I read the words of this particular text, I began to think about many churches that claim to be open in the name of Jesus but are doing nothing about social injustice. This is what the prophet Amos spoke out against in his day, and his prophecy also speaks to us today. In Amos's time, prophets had a special job. Many viewed prophets as people who spoke concerning the future, but the prophets actually did more than that. Walter Brueggemann suggests that "the prophet must speak evocatively to bring the community the fear and the pain that individual persons want so desperately to share and to own but are not permitted to do so. The prophet does not scold or reprimand."[49] The prophet speaks so that people will look at and understand gross injustice that is not being addressed. So often today, God needs a voice to rise from the pulpit to make His people aware of social injustice.

In the text, Amos makes a bold statement concerning camouflaged religion in his day. In simple terms, God was not pleased with worship in the sanctuary because it consisted of mere activity. I believe that in this present day and time, God is still displeased with our activity-centered worship or camouflaged religion. As I first read this passage of Scripture, God immediately revealed to me true elements of real worship.

As I investigated the text, I found that there was a problem with worship in Amos's church, and the prophet adamantly spoke out against it. He used such strong language in the text as "I hate," "I despise," and "I will not." These were phrases directed at the worship or camouflaged religion going on inside the church. Amos allows us to see that the church kept an itinerary; they kept all the right days on their religious calendar. They brought all of the right offerings to the temple for sacrifice. They brought their burnt offerings, cereal offerings, and peace offerings to the temple.

They had the right music, which was sung by the right singers with the right instruments, but God did not listen to them. The people sitting around in the temple heard the songs, but God did not hear them. Many of our activities in the church today are just like those that occurred in the time of Amos, and God is still not pleased with camouflaged religion. J. A. Motyer says, "Their religion was dutiful, exceedingly costly—think of the outlay on animal sacrifices—apparently wholehearted, emotionally satisfying, but if religion does not get through to God, it has failed centrally.[50]

Worship as Acknowledgement

In Amos's time, the people worshipped God outwardly, but their hearts were not right. Their camouflaged religion enabled them to go through the worship experience, but their hearts were not in it. They were just going through the motions. Amos considered how the people celebrated the days, made certain offerings in church, and sang certain songs in the church, while their worship did not acknowledge God. In short, their hearts were not right in their worship experience. Therefore, God closed His nose to the smell of their incense, closed His eyes to their sacrifices, and closed His ears to the sound of their so-called music.

Lloyd J. Ogilvie states,

> God was not impressed by the piping of pious songs while they forgot their responsibility to their fellow women and men, as they grounded the poor into the mire and loaded the overburdened with misery. Burnt offerings that were supposed to be an outward sign of total dedication to God, were a religious mockery; peace offerings affirming fellowship with God were contrary by the people's unwillingness to obey him.[51]

Amos was not concerned about stopping worship itself but more so with the purification of the hearts and the lives of those who worshipped the Lord. And today, like Amos, I have come to report that worship is more than just going through the motions. Worship should be real and sincere, not a mere camouflaged act of the believer. Worship should be more than a bunch of empty rituals lacking the heart and life of the believer.

We must not do away with worship experience, but we must endeavor to experience real worship with dedication and wholesomeness in our lives. The church should not be a big, empty globe of activity but, rather, a real activity that comes from the heart. Real religion should not only acknowledge and worship God in the church but also honor and acknowledge God in daily life after church. Worship is not just coming to church; it is representing God in church and in the world.

Worship as Action

Verse 24 in our text says, "But let judgment run down as waters, and righteousness as a mighty stream" (Amos 5:24 KJV) The New International Version of the Bible says, "But let justice roll on like a river, righteousness like a never-failing stream!" (Amos 5:24 NIV). God wants righteousness and justice in every aspect of life. Thank God for not only the prophet's criticism but also for the positive note here in the text. We can make a change. We do not have to "look" like righteous and justified people when we make our way to the church; we can actually become righteous and justified people. Activity can flow out of the church.

In Palestine, it was common to see streams and rivers that dried up. Many of them dried up in the summer time. I believe that many of our churches are drying up like the Palestine streams and rivers. Therefore, today, I thank God for Amos, the prophet, who gives us a message of hope. Amos helps us to understand that an ever-flowing stream will never dry up.

What kind of activity did God's prophet want to flow out of the church? Page H. Kelley says, "Amos had caught the vision of a just society, a society in which religion was no longer a matter of rites and ceremonies, but a society in which true service to God was service to the poor and the oppressed."[52] In Amos's day, the rich were getting richer, and the poor were getting poorer. There was a great struggle in society between the "haves" and "have nots." Amos impressed upon his brothers and sisters that righteousness and justice should flow out of the church with the power of water in the stream. It should flow as a perennial stream that will never dry up. Justice and righteousness should also fill the land until it overflows.

Every man, woman, and child deserves a fair chance and an opportunity to be treated as a human being. God wants our religion not to be camouflaged but to be openly working to make things better for the poor, sick, oppressed, disenfranchised, hurt, hopeless, and enslaved. God wants us to be concerned about the evil conditions that hurt the lives of so many people—people who don't receive a fair chance. God wants us to work together as a flowing stream to make their conditions better.

God wants the church to be real. He wants the church to care about the poor, widowed, orphaned, powerless, hurt, and helpless, and He wants these concerns to flow actively out of the church. Yes, God wants us to worship in the sanctuary. God wants us to praise Him! God wants us to make sacrifices! However, He also wants us to leave church and serve Him each and every day. The only way we can serve God is through service to one another each day of our existence.

God is not satisfied with mere "outside show," camouflaged religion. He wants inward righteousness that will flow in every aspect of life. God wants righteous hearts from which "justice is like a surging, churning, cleaning stream. All is in motion and commotion. Nothing is at rest."[53] That is what God expects from us, the pastor and the people that make up His church.

Sermon 3: Do You Love Me Enough to Help Me? (Philippians 2:1-2)

Today, let us look at our text in Philippians to gain spiritual insight. After I read the words of the text from the King James Version of the Bible, I decided to look at another translation; therefore, I consulted *The Living Bible*, which has a powerful paraphrase of Scripture. I am certainly blessed by this passage because it seems to speak from the writer's heart concerning social activism. *The Living Bible* says,

> *Is there any such thing as Christians cheering each other up? Do you love me enough to want to help me? Does it mean anything to you that we are brothers in the Lord,*

sharing the same Spirit? Are your hearts tender and sympathetic at all? Then make me truly happy by loving each other and agreeing wholeheartedly with each other, working together with one heart and mind and purpose. —
Philippians 2:1-2 (TLB)

As I read this passage of Scripture, it unfolded in my own mind the significance for the people of faith. This text raises points that can be detrimental to the body of Christ; it also gives insight as to what the body should be. I truly believe that God can bring the body of Christ together on one accord, working with one heart, mind, and purpose.

I am cognizant of the fact that many people do not have joy in serving others or share the idea of being a servant at all. Many people feel that they should receive help but not help others. Many have succumbed to the idea that there is no way for people to come together and work for the common good. I believe it is possible for Christians and the church community to come together and love one another enough to give and receive help. In these dark, difficult, and dangerous times, God is calling pastors and people to make a difference in the lives of all of His people everywhere.

Position

As I read the words of this text, I noticed the word 'if.' It seems the text points out the fact that there may not be, in the church or body of Christ, certain traits or qualities that are needed to help someone. Sometimes as I examine the circumstances, situation, and plight of the world, I wonder if we are truly able to come together and help one another. We are living in a time when rather than coming together, Christians are constantly at one another's throats. This affects people adversely and leads them to say, "If you want to get hurt, come to church. If you want folks to talk about you instead of trying to help you, come to the church."

The church has many of Satan's adversaries who don't come to make things better; instead they come weekly to make things worse. The church is full of people who, if the leader says go left, must go right. The church is full of people who never look for anything positive, but they always look for something negative. Many will argue that it's hard to find love, encouragement, fellowship, affection, and mercy in the church house. Even families that have been able to live together have made their homes a battlefield, with husbands against wives and children against their parents. Our communities are not helping. Instead, they cause hell for those who do not have or lead them to their own destruction.

When we look at the community around our church, if we are honest, we can say that it is hard to give some people a helping hand. I am sure there are some people you simply cannot help. I am sure there are some people who specialize in using people, looking for handouts, and failing to make their own situation brighter. There are many people that do not want to change. Some people are happy being on drugs, alcohol welfare, shacking, sleeping together out of wedlock, having low morals, and repeating a cycle that will eventually lead to their destruction. Yes! There are some people you cannot help because they do not want to help themselves. Some people like living in the gutter and do not want to leave the gutter.

In the *Chicago Sun Times* this week, a law professor at the University of Texas said, "Black people do not have the sense that white people have." Lina Graglia literally said that Blacks and Hispanics cannot compete academically with white students. Graglia said that Blacks are from a culture in which failure is not seen as a disgrace. In my own opinion, this woman made this statement because she feels that our sons and daughters are so stupid and slow that they will never have the sense of a white child. Many people have written our children off. We hear and believe from parents, teachers, and society that black children will never read, write, or do arithmetic.

In response to this, one might ask, "How can you help in the United States where we are below the international level in math?" In an article in the *Chicago Sun Times*, Rosalind Rossi stated, "Indeed the highest scoring Illinois students came from well stocked homes, indicating possible wealth."[54] Many people feel that our young generation today is hopeless and helpless. Church members may ask, "Really, pastor, how do you help a community where half the homes are led by a single mother? How do you help a community where one-third of the people live in poverty? How do you help children that come out of school and are unable to spell grass yet can smoke it?"

Presuppositions

We often speak hypothetically, but in reality improving humanity should be a part of the Christian community. We should want to help people. The church should have certain qualities that show its realness in relationship to the cross. We must be willing to help mankind by bearing our cross in the community. The "ifs" in this text presuppose a quality that ought to be a part of the faith of the community living in unity.

This text points out some ways to create unity. We should cheer one another up instead of tearing one another down. Much of our criticism is not given to help but to hurt. Many people are downtrodden and in need of the church to lift their spirits. The King James Version of the Bible uses the word "consolation" (Philippians 2:1), for which the Greek word is *paraklesis*, variously translated in other New Testament passages as 'comfort,' 'exhortation,' and 'incentive.' There is a sense here that there is meant to be a strong, upholding support in the Christian community.[55] The church is in the business of helping people by cheering them up. Do you know any child or person in the community who needs to be cheered up?

To create unity, we must love one another enough to help one another. The word 'love' is big. Love always looks beyond all of our faults and sees our needs. Anybody can say, "I love you," but love is action. Anybody can say, "You know I love you," but when someone really needs help, if you are able, you are supposed to help. I believe there are many people in your lives and mine who are crying out for help. We need to work to show the love of Jesus. Real love always shows up when people are in need of help. One thing to remember is that when you show love by helping, sometimes you are going to be hurt. Sometimes love looks beyond your own hurt and still wants to help. How in the world can anybody say he or she truly loves you yet make no effort to help you? Do you love me? Do you love me? Well, help me! I need some help. Real love is able to love the unlovable and the unreciprocal.

I am your brother. Does it mean anything to you that we are members of the same family? The question that I have for you today, church, is: Do you really know who your brothers and sisters are? I want to remind you that all of us have a member in our family whom we would like to forget about and would rather not talk about; we would rather act as if this person were dead. God wants us to help our brother. In my family, we may not talk on the phone each and every day, but when a family member is in need, we try our best to be there for him or her to help in any way that we possibly can. Families must stick together. I just want to let you know that "I got your back." Are you your brother's keeper?

The Christian heart is supposed to be tender and sympathetic. The child of God must be willing to show compassion toward his or her brothers and sisters. I know it is easy to say, "I am too busy." But we must learn how to put ourselves in the other person's place and try to feel the pain, hurt, heartache, and burdens he or she is experiencing. As people of God, we must learn how to be tender and sympathetic toward the poor, sick, handicapped, oppressed, disenfranchised, hurt, hopeless, and enslaved. We are supposed to have a heart and a willingness to show compassion for people in need.

Prescription

Listen to the words of verse 2 as I read them from *The Living Bible*: "Then make me truly happy by loving each other and agreeing wholeheartedly with each other, working together with one heart and mind and purpose" (Philippians 2:2 TLB). What a powerful statement this is for the body of Christ today. This verse suggests that wonderful things can happen when people of God come together on one accord. I believe God wants us to come together with one heart, mind, and purpose to love people enough to help them. Paul, the writer of this text, is in jail, but he tells the church how in the midst of his bondage, they could make him happy. Nothing could make a leader as happy as having the people whom he leads come together on one accord. When souls come together and hearts beat together, there can be unity, and the church can start loving enough to help.

If you want to make God's pastor happy, start working together, start walking together, and start giving together. If you love me enough to help me, then let's come together and help the children, mentor the children, and tutor the children. If you want to help me, give of your finances so that we can really begin to build our children's ministry. If you really want to help me, let's use our church as a safety zone and our gym to work with families.

Sermon 4: Looking Out for Others
(Philippians 2:3-4)

Today we want to continue with Paul's letter to the church at Philippi. Paul is writing a letter to the saints and the servants in this particular province. While in prison, Paul received word that there was some strife and contention in the Philippian church. Paul's desire was that the church come together and be on one accord. As a matter of fact, Paul expressed this desire in verse 2: "Fulfil ye my joy, that ye be likeminded, having the same love, being of one accord, of one mind" (Philippians 2:2 KJV). Togetherness in the church would make Paul happy.

The body of Christ should be together on one accord, looking out for others. Many argue that the church of Jesus Christ can't come together, live together, work together, and share. Many say that one of the hardest, most difficult, and most tedious things to do is to get people to work together. In our modern-day society, we can readily see the church and community living apart. Even in times of crisis, rather than work together, the church and community seem to pull farther and farther apart.

Some people in the church argue that it is impossible to look out for others, but I beg to differ. I believe the saints and servants of God can look out for others. In the midst of chaotic times, the people of God can become humble, living without vain conceit and selfish ambition. I believe God is calling His children to live for others as well as for themselves. I believe looking out for others can be achieved through the unity that comes from being one in the Spirit. Let's take a journey through the Word of God and see how we are to live together.

Problem

This text certainly brings out the problems that hinder unity in the body of Christ. It addresses the age-old problem of disunity that is still prevalent in the church today. We, the people of God, should realize that there are certain bad qualities that can creep up on us and become detrimental to the body of Christ. One of these bad qualities is strife.

Paul reveals that there are many factions in the church. In other words, there are often self-seeking spirits that rise up among the people, pushing for positions and ultimately pushing themselves forward. Many Christians today are self-seekers. They always push themselves forward. It seems that in the church today, everybody wants to be "Mr. or Mrs. Important." Some Christians are constantly trying to get up front. They want to be on every committee, lead all of the songs, and have all the church programs going their way. When they are the leaders of a group, they are the best servants in the world, but if somebody else takes the lead, they fight against everything that goes on. Whatever you try to do, they have to add their two cents. They are the only people who are always right and the only ones who know everything. They know how everything inside and outside of the church needs to be done. If they come up with the idea, it is the best thing since sliced bread, but if someone else comes up with the idea, it somehow does not make sense.

These Christians have a Burger King mentality of having it "my way." This sort of attitude leads to strife, factions, cliques, and schisms in the body of Christ. We must learn how to have it God's way instead of our way. A negative attitude has nothing to do with God; it has to do with self. Negativism only hurts the unity of the church and keeps the church from looking out for others.

The Word of God calls self-pride vainglory or conceit. Many people that come to the church are conceited and really feel that they are "it" in humanity. Many do not get big heads until they come to the church. They have a big ego when it comes to their roles and responsibilities in the church. When they come to the church house, suddenly they come up with an enormous pride that brings about some self-imagined excellence. Many people believe the church cannot function without them, for such an inadequate group cannot make it without them.

If you are this conceited, I dare you to die. I guarantee you the church of Christ will march on. So often people feel they are the only ones with certain abilities. They are so quick to say, "I want it done right." Really? Who told you that you were so right? You may be following somebody who has been wrong for years.

Pride makes a person put himself at the center of things. When this happens in the church, it becomes full of competing centers; each one promoting himself, or as Paul put it, his own interest.[56] — **Malcolm O. Tolbert**

I wonder if people will ever learn that they are not important. Jesus and what He commands is important. It is not about you; rather, it's about Jesus being at the forefront. This is not your stage. It is the Lord's stage, and He is the only star.

Prideful

The wrong attitude is one of pride. The right attitude is one of humility. Humility for the child of God is not weakness but strength. The Philippian church was a church and people who needed humility. As A. T. Robertson says:

> The Jewish element had the pride of privilege, the gentile element had the pride of culture. The Pharisee was an egotist and a partisan by inheritance of seclusion virtue and grace. The cultured Greek or the oriental Gnostic had a profound sense of his own superiority over the outside barbarians.[57]

One can see clearly why the people of this church had to humble themselves and come together. Paul brings this point out in Romans 12:3 when he says, "not to think of himself more highly than he ought to think; but to think soberly, according as God hath dealt to every man the measure of faith" (KJV). We are all sinners who have been saved by grace. Humility allows us to lower ourselves and lift others up. Our humility should encourage us to pull our big egos down and esteem others even higher than ourselves.

One of the fallacies in the church is that one person is better than others. Some folks think that God made them great and forgot others. Until you come down off your high horse, you will never be able to look out for others. Rather than pushing for yourself, humility causes you to push your brother. Remember that when you know who you are and what you are, you have no problem coming down and looking out for someone else.

I read a story about an early church father recently re-named Ambrose. He lived his life being kind and looking out for others, which made people look up to him as a father. The church's bishop died, and the people cried out for Ambrose to be the new bishop. He ran away in the night, for he was not looking for the office. The emperor stepped in, and Ambrose became the new bishop. He was a humble man and a great bishop. He realized that the only way to go up is first to come down; then God will lift you up. The way to go up is not to push for yourself but to humble yourself and let God take you up.

Partnership

Abraham Maslow has a theory that supports the need to look out for others. His theory states, "We need to look out for others." His study was centered on people who were happy and doing well. Maslow "developed a theory called self-actualization, and described a composite person whom he designated self-actualized."[58] This kind of person's life is complete when he or she moves beyond the "I, me, and mine" syndrome. This applies to the man, woman, boy, or girl who lives a life beyond "self." I dare you to start looking out for others. I dare you to start reaching out to help others.

Let us look at verse 4, which says, "Look not every man on his own things, but every man also on the things of others" (Philippians 2:4 KJV). This confirms that we should look out for others. We should stop being so selfish. We ought to care about those around us. If we claim to be a part of the body of Christ and all we care about is me, myself, mine, and I, we are headed for trouble. We don't exist alone in the church or in the world, so we must learn how to look out for one another. Life is more than just your own way; it is also the way of others.

We must be socially active in trying to make things better for our brother. Social activism means to work to make things better for the poor, sick, handicapped, oppressed, disenfranchised, hurt, hopeless, and enslaved. We need for others to look out for us. We should also look out for others. We should look out for someone who is crying out for help. "We must look! Look! Look!"

Sermon 5: The Mind of Christ Jesus (Philippians 2:5)

This is our third in the series of Paul's message to the church at Philippi. As I read this passage of Scripture, I realized that the apostle was stressing unity within the body of Christ. Paul was in jail, and he wrote a letter to the church that he founded. He helped them realize that they should be together, on one accord, and unified as a people of God. In this text, Paul makes a profound statement: "Let this mind be in you, which was also in Christ Jesus" (Philippians 2:5 KJV).

The older I get, the more I realize that the mind is a terrible thing to waste. The mind gives direction to the whole body. When an individual becomes brain dead, he or she is dead. If the brain is functioning right, it can give directions to every inch of the body. With my brain, I am able to tell my legs to move, eyes to shut, mouth to chew, and arms to move. Every person ought to learn how to develop his or her brain in positive ways. I read recently that a person will only use two percent of the capacity of the brain in a lifetime. In Greek, the word 'mind' is *nous*, which is the seat of reflective consciousness, comprising the faculties of perception and understanding and those of feeling, judging, and determining. In other words, it is that ounce of intellect that determines everything we do and ought to do. You do not exist as a whole person if you do not have a mind.

In this worldly, wicked, and wayward society, is it possible for people to have a mind of Christ Jesus? I realize that so many of our young, middle-aged, and elderly minds have been messed up. Is it possible to teach old dogs new tricks? Do people really want to change? When it comes to finding those who have a mind of Christ, we see so many people that have been wrongly programmed by society and the world at large.

Is it possible to penetrate the deep caverns of these minds and hearts to make them truly want to change and to have a mind of Christ Jesus?

I believe it is possible for a Christian and a church to have the mind of Christ Jesus. I believe that if the people of God will open their hearts to the Spirit of God, they can truly have minds like Christ Jesus that are active in their daily walks of life. Through Paul, God is calling for a society in which people can live with minds like that of Christ Jesus.

Treacherous Mind

When I think of the different minds that people have, I realize that many are treacherous and messed up. In the Philippian church, many minds functioned on a worldly level. This is what breaks the unity in a church. The worldly point of view is to get all that you can and then get some more. In this text, Paul gave some examples of people who have messed-up minds that have been trained by the people of the world. The world tell us that we are number one and we should worry about me, myself, and I. The world's point of view says that instead of looking out for others, you had better worry about yourself.

The world tells us that we need more clothes, bigger cars, more jewelry, more money, bigger houses, and better neighborhoods with few or no black people. The worldly mind says that you can't help anyone. The world tells you that you can't trust any black people; watch your back or get back. If they love you enough to help you, they will surely end up hurting you and making a fool out of you. The world wants you to think that life is a contest and the first person that gets to the top with the most toys wins. The world does not want us to cheer one another up, help one another, care for one another, and have a sense of compassion. The world is concerned about itself and feeding its own ego. What we see today is a world of people with messed-up minds who have somehow messed up society.

Something has to be wrong with our minds when tenants are suing landlords to live in an apartment and shack. People do not care about those with no hope, the homeless, helpless, and hungry. Something is wrong when people don't care for children and will not work to give them a fair chance in life. Something is wrong with minds in America when our elderly have to eat dog food. Something is wrong with minds when we have officials of power in government and church that don't care. It should concern the people of God when brothers and sisters are shot down although they are not bothering anyone. This kind of mindset is what Paul warned the Philippian church about.

Transformed Mind

I've come today to report that God can replace a messed-up mind with a right-spirited mind. The messed-up mind can be replaced with a mind renewed by the power of Christ Jesus. Paul speaks out to the church at Rome, "And be not conformed to this world: but be ye transformed by the renewing of your mind" (Romans

12:2 KJV). The Phillips translation says, "Don't let the world around you squeeze you into its own mould, but let God re-mould your minds from within" (Romans 12:2 PHILLIPS). God wants to reprogram your computer.

One of our problems is that we feed our minds the wrong kinds of information. We watch the wrong kinds of programs. We look up to the wrong kinds of people. We frequent the wrong kinds of places. We read the wrong kinds of books. We hang out with the wrong kinds of people. I believe that God wants us to move from the worldly point of view to the godly point of view. Often when I look at some of the advertising on television, hear it on the radio, and see it in magazines, I feel advertisers are trying to pull us into the bottomless pit of the world.

God does not want our minds conformed to the world's way of thinking. He wants our minds to be transformed and renewed. He wants minds that have been renewed by the power of God. I've come to report today that if you, as a believer, plan to live differently, you must think differently. When your mind has been renewed or transformed, you operate on a different level from people of the world. When a child of God's mind has truly been changed, it shows up in every aspect of his or her life. Saints, are you settling down to the fact that God can renew your mind, or are you an active participant in the renewed mind syndrome?

Transcendent Mind

The text tells us to "let this mind be in you, which was also in Christ Jesus" (Philippians 2:5 KJV). The New International Version says, "Your attitude should be the same as that of Christ Jesus" (Philippians 2:5 NIV). This passage of Scripture is speaking to you and me; Paul is telling us that we need to follow the man called Jesus Christ. He tells us that our minds should be like that of Christ. Paul tells us who God is and what God has called us to do. We should look at Christ as a pattern, picture, and portrait of how we as Christians are supposed to live. Hence, in this scripture, we see Christ as a classic example of the servant that we should be.

There was a fictitious book written many years ago entitled *In His Steps* by Charles M. Sheldon. In this book, a church decided that each member wouldn't do anything without asking him- or herself, "What would Jesus do?" I have come today to tell you that our minds should be fixed on following Jesus. Our attitudes about the things in life should be like that of Jesus Christ. Samuel D. Proctor said:

> The street people, the bag lady, the homeless in our cities are very close to the kinds of people Jesus served here on his earthly ministry. If God were calling us, what would the message say? Will it sound like something Jesus will say also? We are facing the embarrassment of seeing persons who claim to be born again Christians identifying themselves with militarism, and unbridled super patriotism, rejecting the poor, calling for the reversal of civil rights gains, and opposing federal activity that improves life chances for the poor. They speak loudly of being led by the

Holy Spirit. And, yet, so much of what they stand for is alien to the gospel of the good news of God.[59]

My purpose today is to tell you that I believe this is the type of mind and attitude we as believers should have. We must come down in order to be obedient to God. We must come down in order to serve the Lord. I believe that what's on my mind is on your mind. My mind is made up, fixed up, and cleaned up.

I have decided to follow Jesus,

I have decided to follow Jesus,

I have decided to follow Jesus,

No turning back,

No turning back![60] — **Norman Johnson**

Sermon 6: Jesus as a Servant (Philippians 2:6-10)

Today we will continue with Paul's letter to the church at Philippi. During the time of our text, Paul was in jail, and he wrote a letter to one of the churches he founded on one of his missionary journeys. As I read this letter, it certainly appeared to me that Paul was concerned about the lives of the people who were a part of this church as well as their relationships with one another in the total framework of the church.

Paul addresses this letter "to all the saints in Christ Jesus which are at Philippi" (Philippians 1:1 KJV). He refers to the people who make up the body of Christ as "servants." These servants are together because they all belong to the same Jesus Christ. They are supposed to be unified because they are servants of the same master. As I think about the text, I ask myself, "Could someone write a letter to me as pastor, or even to you as a church member, and truly address us as servants of the living God?"

In the church of Jesus Christ, we are His servants. Maybe I should rephrase that to say the people of the church are supposed to be servants of the living God. I have come to the conclusion that most of the people who make up the body of Christ don't have a servant mentality. In the midst of a society where people are so busy and concerned about their own selfish agendas, it is hard to find people willing to be servants of God. Is it truly possible for us as servants to live with the attitude of Christ and be just like Jesus when He walked the streets here on this earth?

I am cognizant of the difficulty in finding servants in this self-righteous, self-satisfied, and self-sufficient world. Today, I have come to share that it is difficult to do anything for Christ without being a true servant. We can worship God and praise Him to the highest, but how many of us are really willing to serve the true and living God? Are we really too busy to serve Him? Or, are we just too lazy and lethargic to serve Him? Are we just too big to come down and serve the Lord?

I believe that it is possible for God's people to take on the role of a servant. I believe that people can change and become truly effective servants who serve God by serving others both in church and in their everyday lives. I believe that even today, in a world with so many problems and difficulties, it is possible to be true servants. The devil must not be allowed to write a death certificate for the church for lack of servants because God can elevate and appoint people who will serve Him until death. They will serve not only with their mouths or voices but also with their whole bodies and souls.

As we look at this passage of Scripture, we can see that Christ was truly a servant. Dr. George McRae of the Mt. Tabor Baptist Church of Miami, Florida, said (in one of our meetings), "We who make up the church lift up the role of Jesus as a priest and king, but we fail to lift Him up as a servant." This passage of Scripture in Philippians truly gives us the picture and pattern of Jesus as a servant.

Self-Emptying Servant

Jesus held a lofty position of power, prestige, and prominence. I understand that Jesus was truly the Son of God. Let us remember that He is still God, for He and the Father are one. Remember that Jesus will always be co-existent, co-equal, and co-eternal with God. Jesus was in the highest position that one could ever attain. He was sitting at the right hand of His Father's throne. He "thought it not robbery to be equal with God" (Philippians 2:6 KJV). The New International Version puts it: "did not consider equality with God something to be grasped" (Philippians 2:6 NIV).

Jesus could have held on to His place in glory, but He was willing to come down. Ask yourself, "Who would want to leave Jesus' home and come to this wicked earth?" He came from His lofty position to be a servant. To be a servant, He exchanged heaven for earth, golden streets for dust, glory for a cross. He came down. Jesus was willing to surrender power in His heavenly position to tend to a difficult task here on earth.

I believe that Jesus is speaking to us right now, saying, "I was willing to leave glory to become incarnated and live here on earth." He was willing to come down. Are you willing to come down? Look at His paradigm: Jesus was willing to give up His rank, rights, power, and privilege to come down to earth. He could have held on to His high status, but He came down to serve. He should be our example and motivation for coming down to serve. Are you willing to follow Christ and come down in your committees, groups, families, with your spouse, and in your church to serve?

Humble Servant

For Christians to be true servants, they must learn to humble themselves. If Jesus could humble Himself and become a servant, why can't we follow His example? The Bible says Jesus "took upon him the form of a servant, and was made in the likeness of men: And being found in fashion as a man, he humbled himself" (Philippians 2:7-8 KJV). He was not a big shot with a proud-as-a-peacock attitude. He was willing to come down and humble Himself.

Humility is a lowliness of mind. Humility is the grace that makes us think of ourselves without thinking we are Mr. or Mrs. "it." It literally means to be meek. It is a state of mind in which we believe, in the eyes of God, that we have no merits of our own, nor are we bigger and better than our brother. So many people are so high up that they can't serve God. They are so busy serving themselves. One of the biggest problems in the church today is that we are not humble.

I've heard Dr. E. Edward Jones, President of the National Baptist Convention of America, Inc., tell the story about his mother and himself on more than one occasion. He tells of going home to see his mother one day. He began to tell his mother that he was a moderator; president of the Louisiana State convention; president of the National Baptist Convention of America, Inc.; his picture was in *Ebony* magazine, where he was listed as one of the one hundred most influential black leaders. He continued by saying, "Mother, I am the pastor of the Galilee Missionary Baptist Church, which is one of the greatest churches in this country." When he finished, his mother said, "Get down on your knees, boy, and tie my shoes."

He told this story so people could see that even in his high-ranking positions, his mother was keeping him humble so God could still use him. He held all of those positions, but he still had to humble himself before his mother. It is easy for people to become big-headed when God begins to bless them, but sometimes they get so high that God can't use them. Many people cannot handle being at high altitudes because they start getting funny attitudes. Most people are just not willing to come down and be servants for the Lord.

I hope you understand that the Bible tells us Jesus was a servant. To be a servant literally means to be a bond slave. In its Greek origin, slave is *doulos*, which means one who is in a permanent relationship of servitude to another. A servant's will is altogether consumed in the will of another.

Jesus came down and put on humanity the duty to serve one another. He came down from heaven to be a slave for the work of the Kingdom. Not too many people in the church generally have this kind of attitude about serving God. Now, we should be able to understand the words of Christ when He said, "Whosoever will be chief among you, let him be your servant: even as the Son of man came not to be ministered unto, but to minister, and to give his life a ransom for many" (Matthew 20:27-28 KJV).

Obedient Servant

The last characteristic that Christ gives us of a servant is His obedience. The Bible tells us that Christ "became obedient unto death" (Philippians 2:8 KJV). How many people are willing to be obedient to the Lord? The mark of a slave is obedience. How many of us here today are truly obedient to the Lord? Now remember, He was obedient unto death. He could have called angels to deliver Him. He could have spoken the word, and the people who crucified Him would have been killed on the spot. Remember that He was obedient unto death, not to death. Jesus' death on a horrible hill called Calvary did not stop Him from being obedient to the Father. He was willing to be obedient, even if it meant that He would die the way criminals died, by crucifixion. Today, I've come to tell you that the limits and boundaries for any and all true servants is death on the cross. Jesus was willing to serve even when it meant death on the cross by the hands of notorious criminals.

If you truly want to be a servant, you should take up your cross. Bearing your cross is a means of social activism. If we are going to be true servants of the living God, we must bear the cross to help our church, community, and children. We must also bear the cross to help the poor, sick, handicapped, oppressed, disenfranchised, hurt, hopeless, and enslaved. That's why I love the words of the song "Must Jesus Bear the Cross Alone?":

Must Jesus bear the cross alone

And all the world go free?

No there's a cross for everyone

And there's a cross for me

The consecrated cross I'll bear

Till death shall set me free

And then go home my crown to wear

For there's a crown for me[61]

— George N. Allen and Thomas Shepherd

Sermon 7: The Light of the World
(Philippians 2:14-16)

Paul, the apostle, is writing a letter to the church at Philippi emphasizing one of his recurring themes of church unity. Paul speaks out and tells the Philippians that they must love one another and help one another. Paul wants this to be a church whose members will look out for one another. Paul reminds them that their minds and attitudes should be the same as Christ's. To put all of this in perspective, he gives a great kenosis scripture that explains to us the perfect example of what a servant of the Lord looks like. Paul's message is to the Christians at Philippi and all believers of today. Paul reveals to this church that they are the light of the world.

This passage of Scripture should remind us that we who make up the body of Christ are truly the light of the world. This is a recurring theme in the Word of God. Throughout the Scriptures, we see that Christians are symbolized as the true light of the world. Yes, there are some problems with many of our lights. Many believers' lives are so dark that they do not shine or look like light to the world. I've come in contact with many people who don't display the kind of light that Jesus is calling for in these last and evil days. In fact, many Christians and churches are living lives that bring darkness to the body of Christ.

I believe what Jesus said: "Let your light so shine before men, that they may see your good works, and glorify your Father which is in heaven" (Matthew 5:16

KJV). It is still possible for the body of Christ to let its light shine for the community and the children to see. Our light can shine and help move the darkness of sin, shame, and Satan and the gloom that he has put on the world today. I believe that the people of this Christian community of which I am a servant can make a change and truly begin to let our light shine for the world to see. Let's look at the text to get a better view of how we can let our light shine. Let's examine this scripture so that we may apply it to our daily lives.

Darkness of the World

In verse 15, Paul describes the world as "a crooked and perverse nation" (Philippians 2:15 KJV). It doesn't take much for us to see that we are living in a world that is crooked and perverse. The word 'crooked' describes people who live with crooked minds, crooked hearts, crooked lives, and crooked actions. It describes people who follow crooked paths, crooked steps, and crooked ways. It describes a people who are bent on going in all of the wrong directions instead of the right one. Paul also tells us that the world is perverse. The word 'perverse' means to warp, twist, corrupt, distort, and pervert. In short, it means to turn away. This suggests to me that the Philippian people had turned away from God's way to other ways of life.

As I thought about the words of this text, it was easy to understand how a crooked and perverse nation acts. The New International Version of the Bible calls the Philippians "a crooked and depraved generation"

(Philippians 2:15 NIV). I can certainly relate our crooked, bent, perverse, distorted, and topsy-turvy world to the Philippians in Paul's day. The more I look at our society, the more I realize that people are moving further away from God. The more I look at this nation, the more I see how people and places are moving further away from God.

I look at some people who used to respect God; now they don't even respect themselves. Some people used to respect the church, and now they don't even care about it. This seems to be a world in which individuals rob their own mothers to buy drugs. In this cruel world, people beat and rape senior citizens. This world spends billions of dollars on bombs and defenses yet doesn't care about the homeless, hungry, helpless, and hopeless. In this world, the "haves" don't care about the "have nots." People leave newborn babies in garbage cans. Individuals would rather drink alcohol, snort cocaine, pop pills, and shoot up drugs than eat.

This world builds casinos for poor people to dream about winning fortunes while they only end up losing money for their cars and homes. This crooked world likes to label wrongdoing as right and vice versa. Individuals stuck in traffic would rather walk up to your car and blow your brains away than wait. This world has too many people that are beating little babies to death. Today, many times one has to look twice because one doesn't know what lies beyond a person's appearance. It does not take a genius to see that people of this world are crooked in church, in the White House, and even in your house.

Darkness of Witness

In the midst of a crooked and perverse world, it is important and crucial that the believer is not a witness of darkness. It is no mistake that here in this text, the Apostle Paul presents some qualities and characteristics that should not be present in the believer because they would dim the witness of his or her light to the world.

In verse 12, Paul tells the Philippian church to "work out your own salvation" (Philippians 2:12 KJV). I know all of you have read Ephesians 2:8, which states, "For by grace are ye saved through faith; and that not of yourselves: it is the gift of God" (KJV). This letter allows us to see that salvation is free because of the salvific work of Christ. We can see that it is a gift for anyone to accept Jesus Christ as his or her Lord and Savior. However, one might question the expression "work out your salvation." In reality, Paul wants the actions of our salvation to grow in our lives. Salvation is free, but somehow we must be willing to follow Him and grow in His Spirit.

So many people join church just to put their names on the church role, but their lives never exemplify that they are children of God, believers, who have been saved and born again. The church should give continual evidence that they are children saved of the King. The process of sanctification must be at work in the believers, making them grow better and stronger each day. We can do this in great numbers by humbling ourselves before God and placing His desires first. As we grow closer to God, we should continue to follow Him and not stray.

> The believer is called to self activity, a pursuit of the will of God, to the promotion of the spiritual life in himself, to the realization of the virtues of the Christian life, and to the personal application of salvation.[62] — **Jac J. Muller**

This whole process is God at work in the believer, with His Holy Spirit working in and through the believer's life.

According to verse 14, another way for the children of God to darken their witness to the world is by "murmurings and disputings" (Philippians 2:14 KJV). In the church, many of us are busy murmuring and disputing. True Christians are servants of God and shouldn't murmur or mutter solemn discontent. Disputing Christians who always question God, inwardly and outwardly, are not desired. Even Paul expresses dissatisfaction at the sight of fussing and fighting believers.

The Israelites who were in the wilderness with Moses had the same problems of murmuring and disputing. These people of God had a stubborn spirit. Have you ever seen people who, no matter what you as a pastor or president are trying to do, always feel the need to add their two cents? They just have to keep up some hell. Most of these people have not submitted themselves to God but answer to themselves. There are many discontented, questioning, and grumbling people in the church who claim to be saints of God. In the tabernacle in the wilderness, this is how the people of God acted with Moses. Their negative actions were really against God because Moses was His representative.

The Christian should not live in darkness, acting in unjust and unrighteous ways, without remorse. God wants His children to have a life that is blame-free and innocent, without a blemish. Our lives should be more pleasing to God; we should not show the world a lot of flaws when they look at us in the church. Christians should have the right action, which comes from having the right motive. In short, we must walk upright and hold up the light.

The Light of the World

The Word of God tells us that we are to "shine as lights in the world" (Philippians 2:15 KJV). Just as Jesus is the light of the world, we, His children, must also let our light shine. The world doesn't need any more darkness; it needs light. Light will always push darkness aside. Light always makes a difference to a world that is crooked and perverse.

A few weeks ago, I came home from church, and the power was out in my neighborhood. My wife and children were sitting in the dark house because there was no power; there was no light. Our TV, VCR, radios, air conditioner, washer, dryer, and garage door would not work. I couldn't see where to put my key in the door. Because there was no power, there was no light. Thank God we are hooked up to the power source. I'm thankful that God has given every child a light.

On September 7, 1994, lying in a casket at Gatling funeral home on Chicago's south side was a young boy named Robert "Yummy" Sandifer. Robert had fired shots from a gun in a gang fight and killed a fourteen-year-old girl. Members of his own gang shot him twice in the head to stop him from squealing to the police about his gang affiliation.

This young man had obviously seen no light. His world was crooked and perverse. His father was locked up in jail. His mother was the third child of ten, four with different fathers. She had her first child out of wedlock at age fifteen, and now at twenty-five she had a total of five children. She was arrested forty-one times on charges of prostitution. Yummy, as he was called, died at the age of eleven with twenty-three felonies and five misdemeanors. This child lived in darkness because he never saw light.

There is a great need for the church to be the light for those who are poor, sick, handicapped, oppressed, and hopeless. We have to thank God for some Christians who let their light shine for the world to see. The Bible tells us, "Ye are the light of the world. A city that is set on an hill cannot be hid" (Matthew 5:14 KJV). The Bible says, "Let your light so shine before men, that they may see your good works, and glorify your Father which is in heaven" (Matthew 5:16 KJV). The Bible tells us, "For ye were sometimes darkness, but now are ye light in the Lord: walk as children of light" (Ephesians 5:8 KJV).

We should shine like stars in our dark world. We must be a light for people. People who are on life's highway should be able to follow the light. If a person is lost on the roadside, some Christian with a light should say, "Get back on the road and follow me." Thank God for Christians and churches that are light and beacons for the Lord. I have decided that I will be one of the lights in the world.

> This little light of mine, I'm going to let it shine
>
> Every where I go, I'm going to let it shine
>
> All in my house, I'm going to let it shine
>
> I'm not going to make it shine, I'm just going to let it shine
>
> Out in the dark, I'm going to let it shine
>
> Let it shine, let it shine, let it shine.[63]
>
> — Lillian M. Bowles

Sermon 8: Repairing the Breaches (Isaiah 58:12)

Today's text is found in Isaiah 58:12. The prophet Isaiah is the speaker. Isaiah's message of restoration speaks to his own times as well as to our times. Isaiah speaks much in the same way as his contemporaries, Amos and Micah. He boldly speaks his message of utmost importance for the people of God to repair the breaches. Isaiah's audience is made up of a group of people who were so religious that they failed to realize what true religion was all about. God always has a spokesperson to inform people of their shortcomings, even those in the religious realm.

Isaiah spoke out in the midst of problems and gave a message of hope and deliverance. Often Christians are told they are "good people," but Isaiah told church people that they were not "good people." In fact, he admonished them to change, grow, and learn. The focal point of Isaiah's message to the church of his day and the church of our day is "Repairing the Breaches." Let us consider Isaiah's call to restoration in our text.

As I meditated upon this passage of Scripture, I became keenly aware that many breaches in society ought to be repaired. There are many breaches within the family structure, marriages, and society as a whole that are in need of restoration. There are breaches in our churches as well as in our communities. With God as our leader, I believe we can be used as vehicles to help in the process of repairing the breaches and restoring a sense of wholesomeness to our homes, churches, and communities.

Some argue that this world has become a hopeless situation. They believe society has become so bad that there is no way to make a true change. They see gaps and tears they believe cannot be patched, fixed, or repaired. They often say, "Before it gets any better, it will get worse." Some say it's useless for anyone to invest time, energy, and money into people who are continually destroying themselves every day with every chance they get. I know there is a large percentage of Christians who argue that some people, places, and things can never be changed, but I believe that with the help of God, breaches can be repaired. I believe that with God in the picture, restoration is attainable. I don't think it's too late for generations of people to change.

Ruin

As I read this text, I became aware of the troubles in Isaiah's time. Through Isaiah, we are able to see the catastrophic, calamitous, unfavorable, and unfortunate conditions of his homeland. During this time, one could look at the physical structures of the land and see the impoverished conditions. The temple, with all of its beauty and magnificence, needed rebuilding. The walls, which once stood as a picture of power, had fallen apart. Many of the city houses had been destroyed, and people had resorted to living in their basements. The streets, where fine chariots and purebred horses traveled, were in dire need of repair. One could see that someone should come forth and repair the breaches in the land.

In addition to the land's physical condition, there was also a breach in the people's spirituality. They indulged in sin without shame. They engaged in activity without action. Even though the temple hadn't been rebuilt, people continued with all the outward motions of fasting and praying, yet their lives were removed from God. In this time period, fasting and praying were outward signs to show the world that the church people in Isaiah's day were religious. Ironically, while they were showing outward signs of religion, their hearts and lives were far away from God.

Like the church people of Isaiah's day, I believe that many times we are guilty of going through the motions with religion when our hearts are not right. In the church, there are many Christians who live in ruin and need their lives restored. Many look holy at church, but when they leave the church, their lives are full of hell. Every once in a while this hell slips out even in the church and causes strained or broken relationships. Christians should stop blaming one another for their own faults and realize that they are leading themselves to destruction because of the breach in their religion.

Our communities are falling into ruin more and more each day. The housing conditions of many people are pathetic. Society too often abandons our senior citizens. Our communities are full of deadbeat dads who walk away from their children. There are far too many young black boys caught in the clutches of drugs and inadequate education, only to end up in jail cells with people who further educate them in crime life. Funeral directors are busy burying not old people but young people who haven't even had a chance to live. Too many mothers are crying at their own children's gravesides. Young girls are still having babies out of wedlock. The family structure has been torn apart by sin, divorce, and ungodly lifestyles.

Here are some astounding statistics that show us how much we need to repair the breaches in black communities:

In 1930, blacks were 22.4 percent of the prison population. In 1986, they were 45.3 percent. In 1990, blacks committed

> 53.9 percent of the murders in America, 63.9 percent of the
> robberies, and 24.3 of rapes. One out of every five black
> men will be incarcerated for a part of his life! Parallel to
> the increase in crime, another breach is paramount: 1950,
> 16.8 percent of Black births were out of wedlock, and
> women headed 17.2 percent of black households. In 1990,
> both of those figures had more than tripled.[64] — **Samuel
> D. Proctor**

These figures clearly give us an indication of the
chronic breach in our communities. The lowest statistic
was rape. The black race does not have to rape because
sex is given away without any charge. In our church
community, we see all of the above breaches on street
corners as we travel to the house of the Lord.

Recognition

As I looked at this text, I realized that in order to
repair our breaches, some of our people must come to
understand that some things are not right for them.
Reading the twelfth chapter of Isaiah, I clearly
understand that the people of Isaiah's day were going
through the motions of fasting because their hearts were
not right. They fasted and prayed yet totally opposed
their fellow man. God wanted them to recognize that
they needed to stop their hypocritical fasting because it
was nothing more than an outward show. They had to
recognize that they ought to stop pointing fingers at other
individuals and point out their own sins and
shortcomings. They needed to realize that they had some
fingers pointing back at them. They fasted but did not

reach out to those who were truly in need. Moreover, these church people constantly quarreled and fought among themselves when they should have been worshipping God.

The prophet speaks to them and to us in verses 6 and 7 of chapter 58. He says that if you truly want to fast, help those who are oppressed, the least, the lost, and the left out. If you want to repair the breach, if you want to live a godly life, feed those who are hungry. He proclaims that we can repair the breach by clothing the naked. Some of us have closets so full of clothes that we could not get into them at gunpoint, yet we continue to fast and pray without repairing the breach of selfishness. Fasting without caring for people who are helpless, hungry, and hopeless is not the right spirit.

As I think about the ministry of my church and myself as shepherd, I am forced to recognize some things in my life. Like Jonah, I ran from the calling when I was about twelve years old and did not want to be a preacher. I ran from God, but I could not hide. I looked at the lives of my grandfather and my own father, who were both preachers, and decided that I did not want to preach. However, there was something embedded in me from the Word of God and these two living examples in my family that caused me to surrender to God's call.

Reverend Jim Taylor, along with his children, living in the racist South, helped a white widow raise her sons by working in the fields together. Some members of this white family call my grandmother "mother" to this day. This vivid example of how my grandfather repaired the breach has continued to have a great impact on my spiritual life throughout the years.

My father had a dream. He was a social activist. He died without having his dream become a reality. When he came to Chicago with his pointed shoes and white socks to pastor the St. Paul Missionary Baptist Church, he walked proudly door to door, spreading the gospel. This is why the Harper family is a member of the church today. There are many people still here today because of my father's evangelistic efforts. He believed in making a difference in the lives of young people. That is one reason that he built a gymnasium and a tiny tot day-care center in the church. Chris Bentley was the first child to attend the day care, and he is still a part of the church. He has graduated from college and has continued to keep his life clean. Chris has been successful in life because my father wanted to repair the breach by helping young people build a firm foundation so they could live godly lives.

My father went through life trying to repair the breach by making life better for the poor, sick, handicapped, oppressed, disenfranchised, hurt, hopeless, and enslaved. He built a sixty-unit apartment building down the street from the church but was forced to give it up because some people did not share in his vision. Consequently, his dream didn't become a reality. Nevertheless, determined to repair the breach in his day, he became an entrepreneur; he started a small construction company to help pastors build churches. My father did not make much money from his construction company because his primary goal was to help others. After his death, one of my uncles stated, "The Construction Company was mere charity work because my brother was not charging churches what was needed to make the standard profit in this industry." In his company, my father provided jobs for people who were not able to get jobs with big, established white construction companies.

May God bless my father for his efforts to repair the breaches as he now resides on the other side of the Jordan River. I know he must wonder if his middle child will ever lead this congregation to stop playing church and truly become socially active. Motivated by my father and the Word of God, I find myself being called upon to make a difference in the world. Church, I report to you today that once you recognize who you are and what you must do, you can help to repair the breaches. Once we recognize what God is calling us as a Christian congregation to do, we will truly be able to repair the breaches.

Repair the Breaches

St. Paul, God is calling us as a pastor and people to help repair the breaches. If we get our hearts and lives right with God, we will truly be able to make a difference. I believe that once we get ourselves together, we can help to fix society by repairing the breaches. To repair means to restore, reconstruct, and reform. It means to fix what is broken. I believe that we are not supposed to sing and shout in the church and leave to be idle. I believe that God wants to use us in order to make a difference in the old, wasted places. In my opinion, we shouldn't allow this community to continue to fall, but somehow we must let God use us in order to make a difference.

The places that are wasting away shouldn't continue to disintegrate. I believe we can stop another generation from giving their lives to failure, defeat, and foolishness. I believe that we can touch some children and help them to succeed in life. I believe that we can develop a successful tutoring program. I believe that all of these bright young minds can be helped so that our children can read, write, and excel in all subjects. I believe that we can repair the breaches by having holy men and women become mentors to young boys and girls. I believe that we can adopt the Hinton Elementary School and stand in the gap for some of the children attending this school.

I believe our gym can be used as a safety zone to help keep young people off the streets. I believe that we can provide different kinds of recreation for our youth and adults. I believe that our health ministry can grow. I believe that we can have a successful clothing ministry. I believe that we can feed people living in poverty. I believe that we can build low-income housing and housing for senior citizens. I believe we can have a credit union and teach people to budget and invest their money wisely instead of not ever saving a dime.

Then, we can be called a repairer of the breaches! Then, we can be called the restorers of the path. Can we do it? Can we make a difference? Can we save generations, families, homes, and people? I believe. I believe.

Chapter 4 Notes

We Come to Church to Worship, and We Depart to Serve

I am convinced that purpose is of such vital importance to all a preacher does that it ought to control his thinking and actions from start to finish in the preparation and the delivery of sermons.[65] — **Jay E. Adams**

The goal of this project was to use the power of the preached Word through sermons designed to solicit a response to social action. I strongly believe that there is power in the Word of God. I had no doubt that the sermons I preached would move the people to become socially active. The pulpit has always been a source of inspiration and information that can lead people to higher heights. Throughout the annals of time, preaching has changed those who have heard the Word in their hearts.

When I reflect on my life as the child of a preacher, I realize now how important preaching was in my past and will be in the future. I live to preach the gospel, but I am cognizant that preaching is more than simply expounding on a biblical text. Preaching is more than dealing with the emotions of those who hear the Word. I've heard many great preachers at various conferences and conventions, and I have taken several courses in preaching at the seminary level. However, I realize that I have not "arrived" as a preacher and that the biggest room in my life is the room for growth. Nevertheless, I do have a firm conviction that the preached Word is a key to social activism.

After realizing that my number one gift was preaching, I set out on a journey. This journey encouraged me to look at members of the St. Paul Missionary Baptist Church, where I serve as pastor. I encountered apathy or a lack of interest in social activism among the members of the congregation. With this realization, I set out on a journey to deal with my belief in the power of the pulpit. My mentor, Dr. George McRae, expressed that "anything you want to do in the church starts in the pulpit." He encouraged me to test my hypothesis that preaching could really move the congregation that I serve toward social activism. I had strong belief and conviction about the power of the preached Word, so I set out to critically assess my conviction, not knowing what the final outcome would be.

Accordingly, I developed a methodology of three different phases of action research. The first phase was the pretest survey. This test was developed by the researcher and the contextual associates and critiqued by a consultant. This survey was designed to discover where the congregation was in regard to social activism. The second phase of this project was geared toward a treatment through eight sermons in order to move the congregation toward social activism. Using a questionnaire, the researcher also tested the sermons' effect on a group of contextual associates. The last phase of this project was the post-test survey. The post-test was a duplicate survey of the pretest survey. The researcher compared the results of the two surveys to determine if there was a decrease or increase of interest in social activism.

As I reflect on the obstacles I encountered in trying to arrive at a conclusion or evaluation, I realize first of all that the number of respondents in my post-test decreased. This is just one of the problems I encountered along the way. In the beginning of the project, 192 people agreed to complete a pretest and post-test survey. However, I received only 153 respondents for the post-test. Therefore, the rate of return is 80 percent. This is a good percentage, but 90 percent would have been better. From this documentation, I gather that 39 respondents did not take the post-test, and many were not present to hear all of the sermons.

Another problem I encountered was that many respondents did not truly listen and follow the directions. Many respondents did not take enough time to fill out all the information on the survey. Many respondents did not report their ages in the spaces provided. Also, much to my surprise, some members still did not feel comfortable sharing their beliefs.

In addition, many older respondents had a problem with illiteracy but were too ashamed to ask for assistance. They refused assistance even though it was offered to anyone who needed it. As a facilitator, I could have reworded some of the questions to provide clarity for all of the respondents.

As I critique my methodology in this project, I believe that I might have achieved more effective results if I had utilized a smaller sample group after each sermon to determine their attitude toward social activism. This would have given a clearer indication of what was happening after each sermon was preached.

The final limitation that I encountered was designing a system to sample the same group for pretest and post-test. Initially, after people heard the sermons, they were ready to become socially active, but the energy level and enthusiasm that existed initially has since dropped. I feel that what has taken two years to begin will take many additional years to accomplish. Social activism has to be a lifelong commitment between pastor and congregation.

In conclusion, I feel this journey has certainly been fruitful for me as pastor and for my congregation. It has made me think critically about my life and my calling to preach. This project made me aware that from the beginning to the end, preaching must be done with a purpose in mind. I have re-evaluated what ministry is all about and how preaching coincides with leading people to do ministry in the name of Jesus Christ and follow Him as a servant.

Reflecting upon St. Paul's apathy toward social activism two years ago, I feel that this project has changed their outlook on what ministry is about. Moreover, it has caused many of my members to look at their lives and compare them to the life of Jesus to see where they have fallen short as Christians.

I am cognizant that some members of the congregation were not affected because they resisted change due to dissatisfaction with their own lives as Christians. In contrast, some people were more receptive to this project than they have been to any other project that I have initiated in over twelve years as pastor. Therefore, I believe that our church will live out the mission of following Jesus Christ, who was a social activist.

Projects that I have dreamed about are now truly being planned and implemented by the people of God at St. Paul. We are no longer simply talking about problems; we are now trying to solve the problems. I believe that we are working to make social activism a living reality. "We come to church to worship, and we depart to serve" is taking on new meaning for us.

I have evaluated the preaching part of the project; however, I feel that it would be beneficial to have someone examine the ministry phase of the project. For instance, what types of ministries can be started for communities in crisis? What can happen after preaching social activism from the pulpit?

Notes

1. Smith, Kelly Miller. *Social Crisis Preaching.* Macon, GA: Mercer University Press, 1984. p. 17.
2. Carter, Harold A. *The Preaching of Jonah.* Elgin: Progressive Publishing House, 1981. p. 5.
3. Chicago Fact Book Consortium, ed. *Local Community Fact Book: Chicago Metropolitan Area.* Chicago: Chicago Review Press, 1984. p. 175.
4. "Race and Ethnicity in Englewood, Chicago, Illinois." *Statistical Atlas.* Cedar Lake Ventures, Inc. 22 April 2015. http://statisticalatlas.com/neighborhood/Illinois/Chicago/Englewood/Race-and-Ethnicity
5. Jones, Miles Jerome. *Preaching Papers.* New York: Martin Luther King Fellow Press, 1995. p. 47.

6. Proctor, Samuel D. *Preaching about Crisis in the Community*. Philadelphia: Westminster Press, 1988. p. 80.

7. Fosdick, Harry Emerson. *On Being Fit to Live With*. New York: Harper and Brothers, 1946. p. viii.

8. Proctor, Samuel D. *Preaching about Crisis in the Community*. Philadelphia: Westminster Press, 1988. p. 121.

9. Proctor, Samuel D. *The Certain Sound of the Trumpet: Crafting a Sermon of Authority*. Valley Forge, PA: Judson Press, 1994. p. 16.

10. Smith, Kelly Miller. *Social Crisis Preaching*. Macon, GA: Mercer University Press, 1984. p. 11.

11. Smith, Kelly Miller. *Social Crisis Preaching*. Macon, GA: Mercer University Press, 1984. p. 32.

12. Smith, Kelly Miller. *Social Crisis Preaching*. Macon, GA: Mercer University Press, 1984. p. 97-98.

13. Smith, Kelly Miller. *Social Crisis Preaching*. Macon, GA: Mercer University Press, 1984. p. 93.

14. Fosdick, Harry Emerson. "What Is the Matter with Preaching?" *Harper's*, July 1928. p. 134.

15. Ryan, Halford R. *Harry Emerson Fosdick: Persuasive Preacher*. Westport, Connecticut: Greenwood Press, Inc., 1989. p. 11.

16. Thomas, Frank A. *They Like to Never Quit Praisin' God*. Cleveland, Ohio: United Church Press, 1997. p. 5.

17. Thomas, Frank A. *They Like to Never Quit Praisin' God*. Cleveland, Ohio: United Church Press, 1997. p. 10-11.

18. Thomas, Frank A. *They Like to Never Quit Praisin' God*. Cleveland, Ohio: United Church Press, 1997. p. 105.

19. Thomas, Frank A. *They Like to Never Quit Praisin' God*. Cleveland, Ohio: United Church Press, 1997. p. 56.

20. White, R. E. O. *A Guide to Preaching*. Grand Rapids: Eerdmans Publishing Company, 1973. p. 42.

21. White, R. E. O. *A Guide to Preaching*. Grand Rapids: Eerdmans Publishing Company, 1973. p. 46.

22. Mitchell, Henry H. *The Recovery of Preaching*. San Francisco: Harper Row, 1977. p. 11.

23. Mitchell, Henry H. *Celebration and Experience in Preaching*. Nashville: Abingdon Press, 1990. p. 53.

24. Walker, Wyatt T. *The Soul of Black Worship: Preaching, Praying, Singing*. New York: Martin Luther King Fellows Press, 1984. p. 7.

25. Taylor, Gardner C. *How Shall They Preach*. Elgin, IL: Progressive Baptist Publishing House, 1977. p. 42.

26. Taylor, Gardner C. *How Shall They Preach*. Elgin, IL: Progressive Baptist Publishing House, 1977. p. 51.

27. Crawford, Evans E. *The Hum: Call and Response in African American Preaching*. Nashville: Abingdon Press, 1995. p. 9.

28. Forbes, James. *The Holy Spirit & Preaching*. Nashville: Abingdon Press, 1989. p. 21.

29. Mitchell, Henry H. *Celebration and Experience in Preaching*. Nashville: Abingdon Press, 1990. p. 146.

30. Harris, Forest E., Sr. *Ministry for Social Crisis*. Macon, Georgia: Mercer University Press, 1993. p. 125.

31. Shockley, Grant S. "Black Pastoral Leadership in Religious Education: Social Crisis Correlates." *The Pastor as a Religious Educator*, edited by Robert L. Brown. Birmingham: Religious Educator Press, 1989. p. 206.

32. Stewart, Carlyle Fielding. *African American Church Growth*. Nashville: Abingdon Press, 1994. p. 22.

33. Proctor, Samuel D. *"How Shall They Hear?"*: *Effective Preaching for Vital Faith*. Valley Forge, PA: Judson Press, 1992. p. 14.

34. Craddock, Fred B. *Preaching*. Nashville: Abingdon Press. p. 17.

35. Moyd, Olin P. *The Sacred Art: Preaching & Theology in the African American Tradition*. Valley Forge, PA: Judson Press, 1995. p. 9.

36. Smith, Kelly Miller. *Social Crisis Preaching*. Macon, GA: Mercer University Press, 1984. p. 96.

37. Brueggemann, Walter. *The Prophetic Imagination*. Minneapolis: Fortress Press, 1978. p. 45.

38. Brueggemann, Walter.

39. Proctor, Samuel D. *Preaching about Crisis in the Community*. Philadelphia: Westminster Press, 1988. p. 77.

40. Smith, Kelly Miller. *Social Crisis Preaching*. Macon, GA: Mercer University Press, 1984. p. 33.

41. Proctor, Samuel D. *The Certain Sound of the Trumpet: Crafting a Sermon of Authority*. Valley Forge, PA: Judson Press, 1994. p. 5.

42. Proctor, Samuel D. *Preaching about Crisis in the Community*. Philadelphia: Westminster Press, 1988. p. 8.

43. Adams, Russell L. *Great Negroes Past and Present*. Chicago: Afro-Am Publishing Co., Inc., 1969. p. 138.

44. Smith, Kelly Miller. *Social Crisis Preaching*. Macon, GA: Mercer University Press, 1984. p. 11.

45. Daniel, W. N. Interview by Joel Damon Taylor. Antioch Missionary Baptist Church, Chicago. 23 Oct. 1996. Tape recording.

46. Fitts, Leroy. *A History of Black Baptists*. Nashville: Broadman Press, 1985. p. 320.

47. Stuart, Douglas. *The Communicator's Commentary Series: Ezekiel, Vol. 18*. Dallas: Word Books, 1989. p. 342.

48. Chicago Fact Book Consortium, ed. *Local Community Fact Book: Chicago Metropolitan Area*. Chicago: Chicago Review Press, 1984. p. 175.

49. Brueggemann, Walter. *The Prophetic Imagination*. Philadelphia: Fortress Press, 1978. p. 50.

50. Motyer, J. A. *The Message of Amos*. Downers Grove: Inter-Varsity Press, 1974. p. 131.

51. Ogilvie, Lloyd J. *The Communicator's Commentary: Hosea, Joel, Amos, Obadiah, Jonah, Vol. 20*. Dallas: Word, 1990. p. 321.

52. Kelley, Page H. *Amos: Prophet of Social Justice*. Grand Rapids: Baker, 1973. p. 85.

53. Limburg, James. *Interpretation: Hosea-Micah*. Atlanta: John Knox Press, 1988. p. 107.

54. Rossi, Rosalind. "State Math scores weak." *Chicago Sun Times*. 17 Sept. 1997. p. 2.

55. Dunnam, Maxie D. *The Communicator's Commentary: Galatians, Ephesians, Philippians, Colossians, Philemon, Vol. 8*. Waco: Word Books, 1982. p. 277.

56. Tolbert, Malcolm O. *Layman's Bible Commentary: Philippians, Colossians, 1 & 2 Thessalonians, 1 & 2 Timothy, Titus, Philemon, Vol. 22*. Nashville: Broadman Press, 1980. p. 22.

57. Robertson, A. T. *Paul's Joy in Christ*. Grand Rapids: Baker Books, 1970. p. 118.

58. Dunnam, Maxie D. *The Communicator's Commentary: Galatians, Ephesians, Philippians, Colossians, Philemon, Vol. 8*. Waco: Word Books, 1982. p. 279.

59. Proctor, Samuel D. *Preaching about Crisis in the Community*. Philadelphia: Westminster Press, 1988. p. 74-75.

60. Johnson, Norman. "I Have Decided to Follow Jesus." *New National Baptist Hymnal*. p. 164.

61. Allen, George N., and Thomas Shepherd. "Must Jesus Bear the Cross Alone?" *New National Baptist Hymnal*. p. 85.

62. Muller, Jac J. *The Epistles of Paul to the Philippians and to Philemon*. Grand Rapids: Wm. B. Eerdmans Publishing Co., 1983. p. 81.

63. Bowles, Lillian M. "This Little Light of Mine." *New National Baptist Hymnal*. p. 401.

64. Proctor, Samuel D. *The Substance of Things Hoped For*. New York: G. P. Putman's and Sons, 1995. p. 174-75.

65. Adams, Jay E. *Preaching with Purpose*. Grand Rapids: Zondervan, 1982. p. 1.

66. Myers, William R. *Research in Ministry*. Chicago: Exploration Press, 1993. p. 65.

Appendix A: Results & Analysis

Field Experience

Church life is full of experiences that provide non-verbal lessons or sermons for one to analyze. As one examines the non-verbal sermons presented by the congregation, one wishes to know the "why" or "how" of these sermons. My experience with St. Paul's non-verbal sermons or their lack of interest in social activism prompted me to verbalize this problem in ministry. As a pastor, I strongly believe that preaching still has power in the midst of the perilous times that we are facing on our Christian journey. It is my contention that the word of God can move people to be a part of social activism. St. Paul's apathy toward social activism perplexes me; the parishioners seem to be going through the motions of worship without caring for their socially disadvantaged brothers and sisters. This action research project therefore grew out of my field experience as a pastor.

As the researcher, I wanted to test the hypothesis of whether or not preaching could produce social activism. In this study the instrument used included a pretest, a sermon series, a post-test, and the sign-up project. These instruments were used as sources of data to evaluate the project.

Along with the contextual associates, who played a key role on this journey, I developed the pretest. The pretest questionnaire was developed in order to determine if the hypothesis that preaching can encourage social activism was valid. After several lengthy discussions, I and the contextual associates identified three areas of concern. These three areas of concern were education, environment, and economics. Our discussion started with concern for the youth as a focus, but it grew to include the entire body of the St. Paul Missionary Baptist church. The survey questions were formulated and subsequently critiqued by Dr. Hill (one of the consultants) who is Professor of Sociology at Chicago State University in Chicago Illinois. After some changes and revisions suggested by Dr. Hill, I was ready to give the survey.

The working title of the project is Operation Restoration: Repairing the Breaches, which is Preaching that Produces the Norm of Social Activism. The survey was given to determine how the members of St. Paul Missionary Church feel about social activism. It was a quick and reliable method to use. In addition, I was able to design this survey to fit this Doctor of Ministry project. The Likert- style scale would be used in this qualitative survey. As I embarked on the journey with this survey, I realized some of the problems that go along with work of this nature. Although this type of survey was most appropriate for generating data in the time period I needed, it still had some probable inadequacies.

As William R. Myers suggests, "questionnaires skim the surface.... They are notorious for low returns.... When too long or too complicated, people rush to completion...and people who are unsure where they stand or interested in sounding radical seek the middle."[66] In spite of these probable inadequacies, however, this method of generating data was deemed most appropriate for this project.

In order to give a survey, a sample group was needed. This group would be open to every member of the church who would participate. Dr. Hill deemed this appropriate because she felt that the more people who participated in survey the better data I would generate. The effectiveness or ineffectiveness of this type of project could be measured more efficiently by a large sample group.

I announced the dates for the pretest survey in my pastoral comments on August 17, two Sundays before it was to be given. On Sunday August 31 and September 7, 1997 I administered the pretest immediately following morning worship service. In order to make sure that the people who took the test felt comfortable and assured of confidentiality, I asked them not to put their names on the survey, but to sign their name on a master list after completing the survey.

Demographics

There were 192 people who participated in the pretest. This number represented approximately 30 percent of the entire congregation. Included in this number were 39 males, 63 females, and 99 people who did not fill in their sex. The different age groups included 27 respondents, age 12-18; 60 respondents, age 19-35; 43 respondents, age 36-49; 47 respondents, age 50-65; 11 respondents, age 66 and older. Four respondents did not check their age on the survey.

The same questionnaire was given as post-test to only 153 respondents. This was due to the absence of 39 respondents who had taken the pretest. They had been instructed before the pretest that their attendance for the pretest, sermons and post-test was important. Nevertheless, the inclement weather on October 26, 1997, and November 2, 1997 (the days of the post-test) prevented 39 respondents from attending church. The total number who took the post-test consisted of 24 males, 67 females, with 62 people not identifying their sex. The age groups included 14 respondents age 12-18; 64 respondents, age 19-35; 37 respondents, age 36-49; 25 respondents, age 50-65, and 10 respondents 66 and older. Three respondents failed to place their age group on the survey.

Survey Results

I now want to focus on some of the survey questions and look at some of the percentages of change from the pretest followed by the treatment of the sermons reflected in the post-test. The questions are 3 through 19.

3. <u>The responsibility to teach young people what they should be taught in public school system should be taught by the church</u>. Those who strongly agreed increased 10.3 percent and those who agreed increased 2.8 percent. This leads me to believe that many more individuals feel that the church should be socially active in teaching and tutoring young people.

4. <u>Part of the mission of the church is to teach young people biblical principles</u>. The respondents who strongly agree increased by 7.2 percent and those who agree increased by 4.0 percent. This question was given in order to determine if awareness for the need to teach young people biblical principles existed.

5. <u>Men of the church should take an interest in young people and help them develop into moral and spiritual people</u>. The number increased by 3.7 percent for the respondents who strongly agree and 3.7 percent for those who agree. This indicates a need for Christian men to be socially active in the lives of young people.

6. <u>Young mothers can benefit from the experiences of older more mature women of the church</u>. There were positive increases of 25.6 percent in respondents who strongly agree and of 6.7 percent in those who strongly agree of 6.7 percent. The researcher contends that the respondents heard a call to social

activism for older women who can share their experience with younger women.

7. <u>Morals and values should be taught through the activities in the church</u>. There was an increase of 6.5 percent in those who strongly agree. This suggests that the sermons made them realize a need for activities that deal with education of morals and values.

8. <u>The church should be concerned about preparing our young people to get a job</u>. The respondents who strongly agree increased by 4.2 percent and those who agree increased by 9.2 percent. The sermons were instrumental in moving people to want to be socially active in preparing young people to get jobs.

9. <u>The church should be concerned about social issues related to young people</u>. The percentage who strongly agree increased by 5.7 percent, and the percentage who agree by 8.4 percent. This increase allows one to see that there has been a positive change in attitudes concerning social issues that young people face in the real world.

10. <u>The church should have recreational activities</u>. The number of people who strongly agree increased by 9.3 percent. This shows that there has been growth in the number of people who feel that the church can be active by having various recreational activities.

11. <u>An area in the building should be used for social as well as academic activities</u>. The percentage who strongly agree increased by 4.4 percent, and those who agree by 5.8 percent. The sermons seem to have had a positive effect on those who heard them.

12. <u>Our teens should receive social, as well as academic, counseling</u>. Those respondents who strongly agree increased by 17.3. It seems that as a result of the sermons the parishioners have a better understanding of the needs of the teens and would like to provide counseling that addresses those needs.

13. <u>Willing to participate in ministries to address issues concerning my community</u>. The number willing to participate showed a 10.9% increase in those who strongly agree and a 5.5% increase in those who agree. This leads the researcher to believe that the sermons made some people more willing to participate in outreach ministries in the community.

14. <u>Willing to participate in seminars and training sessions to prepare for participation in these ministries</u>. There was a positive increase of 8.6 percent in those who strongly agree and an increase of 11.2 percent in those who agree. This shows that there are more people willing to learn and be trained for social activism ministry.

15. <u>The church should help educate our youth in the church and the community with tutoring services.</u>

There was an increase of 14.1 percent in those who strongly agree. This shows that there was an increase in the number of individuals who feel the need for a socially active church providing tutoring services for the church and the community.

16. <u>The church should be concerned about people accepting the Lord as their personal Savior and forget about social, economic and family issues</u>. The number of people who strongly disagree decreased by 9.8 percent. This may be attributable to the fact that the number of people who took the survey decreased by 50%. Overall, this was the only negative response in the survey. I feel that the reason for this response was because of the wording of the question. This sentence should have read: "<u>The church should not only be concerned about salvation, but also about social, economic and family issues</u>."

17. <u>Preaching can change my attitude on any of these statements</u>. There was an increase in those who strongly agree of 6.1 percent and in those who agree of 1.2 percent. This gives an indication that preaching can make a change in people's attitudes.

18. <u>Sermons I hear can motivate me to play a key part regarding social activism</u>. There was an increase of 9.1 percent in those who strongly agree and an increase of 7.1 percent in those who agree. This statistic shows that preaching can move them people toward social activism.

19. <u>How much time I am willing to volunteer per week to improve social activism at our church</u>. There was an increase in the amount of time people were willing to spend volunteering. The one-hour time slot increased by 18 percent, and the 2-hour time slot increased by 24 percent. This is a tremendous gain in the amount of time people are willing to give for ministry after listening to the series of sermons.

Operation Restoration Sermon Series

Designed to solicit a social action response, this sermon series was preached from texts in Ezekiel, Isaiah, Amos, and Philippians and was designed to solicit a social action response. These sermons were preached at the St. Paul Missionary Baptist church on Sunday mornings starting on September 7 and concluding on October 26, 1997. The goal of the sermons was to ensure that members of St. Paul Missionary Baptist Church would become socially active.

As a result of these sermons I received many positive responses that indicated how lives were changed. For example, one member called to ask me, "Is there anything that I can do?" Another member came to my office with tears in his eyes saying, "I want to do something; I just need somebody to show me". A third church member called the office to say how effective the sermons were in encouraging him to try to develop a mentoring program here at church. In retrospect, one area I should have focused on was a small sample group to respond after each sermon. This would have given me a better evaluation of the effectiveness of the entire series of sermons. Also, it would have been a good means of tracking the personal responses of those who heard the sermons.

One method I used to find out if the sermons were accomplishing what I set out to do was to use my contextual associates as a sample group. After I preached the fourth sermon, I gave each of them a questionnaire. The questionnaires were returned to me with no names. The questions were as follows:

1. Have the first four sermons touched your life? One of the associates responded by saying, "Yes! The sermons made me aware of the need to get involved in ministries which affect people inside and outside of the church structure." Another context associate responded with this statement: "Yes. Each sermon standing on its own created in me a desire to forge forward to revive, restore, reestablish and reach out to people and places." All of the responses that I received were positive.

2. Have these sermons led you to want to do something in the church and the community? I received some valuable responses for this question also. One of the associates responded with this statement: "They have increased my desire to work harder to help solve some of these situations that exist" Another associate responded, "Yes, I think it is incumbent upon all believers to perpetuate their species (brother and

sisters) to live up to their potential. The sermons have recommitted me to help those in need."

3. <u>Was the style of preaching helpful in moving you to become socially active?</u> The responses I received from this question were also helpful and encouraging. One of the associates responded, "Yes, in each sermon the style of focusing on social change made me aware of problems and solutions. All action says is be active and committed in serving others." Another contextual associate responded, "Yes, this style of preaching reached the whole church and it motivated and move us to do something."

From all of these responses, one can see how the sermons were able to touch, move and encourage all of those who heard them. As I reflect on these sermons, I can still observe how they have touched our congregation.

Sign-Up Project

After the series of sermons was completed, members were asked to sign up for specific projects. People were to sign up for outreach ministries in different areas, on different days and hours. The sign-up project consisted of nine different areas. The first area was *Evangelizing*, which entails an outreach team that will take to the streets. Those who signed up for Evangelizing also signed up for training to do this type of work, which we entitled Operation: SWAT, or Soul-Winning Action Team. The second area was *Prayer*, an outreach ministry that will be concerned with praying for the sick and shut in and bereaved. The third area was *Fitness*, which relates to aerobics and nutrition. The fourth ministry area for which people could sign up was *My Brother's Keeper*, which deals with helping battered women, feeding the hungry (Operation Care), and providing clothes to those in need (Operation Clothes Closet). The fifth area for which people could sign up was Job Ministry, and the sixth area was Technology, which relates to computers and web page building. The seventh and eighth areas of ministry were *Tutoring* and *Mentoring*. The last area will deal with *Athletes*_and using our gym as a safety zone.

The total number of people who have responded thus far by turning in sign-up sheets is 65. The documentation is incomplete because many people are still turning in their sign-up sheets. To date, 17 respondents have signed up for witnessing (evangelizing), 17 for teaching, 19 for prayer and visitation, 8 for aerobics, 5 for dancing, 4 for nutrition, 13 for battered women, 23 for the feeding program, and 36 for the clothes ministry. In addition, 13 respondents have signed up for job preparation, 11 for computers and web page development, 21 for sports ministry, 32 for tutoring, and 38 for mentoring. Many of the 65 respondents have signed up for more than one area.

Appendix B: Methodology

In this project, the researcher, who is also the pastor of St. Paul Missionary Baptist Church, studied the reasons for the church's lack of social activism. He tested whether or not preaching could produce the norm for social activism. The researcher used a formula to gain the essential data.

First, the researcher solicited data from a pretest that was given to a sample group of 192 members. The sample group completed a Likert-style five-point continuum.

Secondly, the researcher preached a series of eight sermons designed to solicit a positive or negative response toward social activism. A post-test followed immediately. Both the pretest and post-test were quantitative and were used together to generate data to show the effectiveness of the sermons and preaching on the members of the St. Paul Missionary Baptist Church. The final part of the formula used consisted of allowing members of St. Paul to sign up for activities showing their talents in areas where they could provide leadership. The sign-up project was another test of their true commitment to social activism.

The methodology of the total project was broken into three phases. The first stage consisted of the pretest and the post-test. The second phase was the series of sermons preached. The final phase was the ministry sign-up project.

The Pretest and Post-Test

To collect data for this project, the researcher used a quantitative method. This method provided the researcher with clarity in looking at the various attitudes about preaching messages on social activism. However, this method was used with the realization that too strong of a conclusion could be interpreted from the data.

The kind of questionnaire used was the Likert-style five-point continuum. The survey given afforded the participants who took it to choose from five different answers: strongly disagree, disagree, undecided, agree, and strongly agree.

The questionnaire was complied by the researcher and contextual associates. The contextual associates consisted of members of the St. Paul Missionary Baptist Church and were hand picked by the researcher for planning and implementing the model. These nine people were of different age groups and sexes and represented different ministries in the church. The contextual associates group was formed in such a way that other participants within the congregation would not feel threatened regardless of their level of education. In meetings, the contextual associates discovered that most problems within the community were centered on the church.

The survey was centered on three major areas: education, environment, and economics. The researcher and contextual associates constructed twenty-one questions for the survey. The questions were reviewed by one of the consultants, Dr. Joan Hill, because of her specialization in the area of social change. The researcher asked members of the congregation to participate in this project by taking a pretest before the series of eight sermons were preached and a post-test after the sermons were preached. The researcher administered the pretest survey on Sunday, August 31 and Sunday, September 7, 1997. The pretest was given immediately following morning worship, at approximately 1:30 p.m., on both Sundays. The total number of members who participated in the pretest was 192. This group of individuals became the researcher's field test group. To ensure that each survey participant remained anonymous, survey participants were asked not to sign their names, but to put their names on a sign-up sheet when they turned in their survey.

The post-test questions were a repeat of the pretest questions. After the series of eight sermons was delivered, the post-test was given. This test was administered October 26 and November 2, 1997, following morning worship. A list of names of those who took the pretest was printed in the worship bulletin. This was done to ensure that the same group would take the post-test. The total number of individuals who took the post-test was 153, which is a lower number than those who took the pretest. The initial sample group was larger than the final sample group because some individuals were not present for various reasons.

Operation Restoration Sermon Series

The series consisted of eight sermons preached at St. Paul Missionary Baptist Church. The sermons were preached from texts in Ezekiel, Isaiah, Amos, and Philippians and were designed to solicit a response to social action. They were preached to persuade members to address certain social issues.

The first sermon preached was "Hope in the Midst of Hopelessness," from Ezekiel 37:1-9. It focused on many negative social conditions and statistics of which individuals should be aware. It also allowed the congregation to see that regardless of the negativity of any situation, God can use His people to make a difference. If "dry bones" can live, so can the conditions we face as people of God.

The second sermon preached was "Camouflaged Religion," from Amos 5:21-27. This sermon made people aware that real religion consists of more than worship activity; it also requires some service. The sermon focused on encouraging the congregation to realize that God requires more than mere worship.

The third sermon preached was "Do You Love me enough to Help Me?" from Philippians 2:1-2. This message focused on social action, or being willing to help other people along their Christian journey.

The fourth sermon preached was "Looking out for Others," from Philippians 2:3-4. This sermon sought to help individuals realize that they should be socially active by looking out for and caring for other individuals.

The fifth sermon preached was "Mind of Christ Jesus," from Philippians 2:5-7. Its central purpose was to further encourage Christians to imitate the actions of Jesus Christ.

The sixth sermon preached was "Jesus as a Servant," from Philippians 2:8-11. This particular sermon's purpose was to emphasize that Jesus was a servant and all Christians are called to be active servants.

The seventh sermon preached was "Light in the Midst of Darkness," from Philippians 2:12-15. This message expressed that we have been called to the task of letting our light shine in the midst of darkness.

The eighth and final sermon preached was "Repairing the Breaches," from Isaiah 58:12. The purpose of this sermon was to show members that they should be socially active by helping to repair the breaches in society.

The Sign-Up Project

After the sermons were preached, a sign-up project was administered to the congregation. The researcher and the contextual associates developed the sign-up project, which consisted of ministries derived from a survey of talents within the congregation. Following the talent survey, the sign-up project was open to participants' interest and availability in nine different areas: Evangelizing, Prayer, Fitness, My Brother's Keeper, Job Preparation, Technology, Tutoring, Mentoring, and Athletics. All of these concerns came from brainstorming and fluent conversation with the contextual associates. Those who signed up as volunteers for each social action ministry are now developing the ministry in their respective area.

Appendix C: Survey Form

PROJECT TITLE: **BIBLICAL PREACHING THAT ESTABLISHES THE NORM FOR SOCIAL ACTIVISM**

**Please respond to the following statements using the scale below:

> **1=Strongly disagree   2=Disagree   3=Undecided**
> **4=Agree   5-Strongly Agree**

**Other questions should be responded to in the most efficient way.

1. What is your age group?

> 12 – 18 _____   19 – 35 _____
>
> 36 – 49 _____   50 – 65 _____
>
> 66 or above _____

2. Are you:

> Married _____ Single_____
> Divorce_____ Separated_____
> Male _____ Female _____

3. I believe I am active in the social concerns of the community.

> Yes _____ No _____

4. Do you live in the Englewood Community?

> Yes _____ No _____

5. The responsibility to teach young people what they should be taught in the public school system should be taught by the church. 1 2 3 4 5

6. Part of the mission of the church is to teach young people biblical principles. 1 2 3 4 5

7. Men of the church should take an interest in young people and help them develop into
    Moral and spiritual people. 1 2 3 4 5

8. Young mothers can benefit from the experiences of older more mature women of the church. 1 2 3 4 5

9. Morals and values should be taught through the activities in the church. 1 2 3 4 5

10. The church should be concerned about preparing our young people to get a job. 1 2 3 4 5

11. The church should be concerned about social issues related to young people. 1 2 3 4 5

12. The church should have recreational activities. 1 2 3 4 5

13. An area in the building should be used for social as well as academic activities. 1 2 3 4 5

14. Our teens should receive social as well as academic counseling. 1 2 3 4 5

15. I am willing to participate in ministries to address issues concerning my community. 1 2 3 4 5

16. I am willing to participate in seminars and training sessions to prepare myself for participation in these ministries. 1 2 3 4 5

17. I think the church should help educate our youth in the church and community with tutoring services. 1 2 3 4 5

18. The church should be concerned about people accepting the Lord as their personal savior and forget about social, economic and family issues. 1 2 3 4 5

19. Preaching can change my attitude on any of these statements. 1 2 3 4 5

20. Sermons I hear can motivate me to play a key part regarding social activism. 1 2 3 4 5

21. How much time are you willing to volunteer per week to improve social activism at our church.

☐30 minutes ☐1 Hour ☐2 Hours ☐No Time At All

Appendix D: Questionnaire for Contextual Associates

PROJECT TITLE: **BIBLICAL PREACHING THAT ESTABLISHES THE NORM OF SOCIAL ACTIVISM**

1. HAVE THE FIRST FOUR SERMONS TOUCHED YOUR LIFE?

2. HAVE THESE SERMONS LED YOU TO WANT TO DO SOMETHING FOR THE CHURCH AND THE COMMUNITY?

3. WAS THE STYLE OF PREACHING HELPFUL IN MOVING YOU TO BECOME SOCIALLY ACTIVE?

Appendix E: Talent Survey

St. Paul Missionary Baptist Church

6954 South Union Avenue

Chicago, Illinois 60621

REVEREND JOEL D. TAYLOR, PASTOR

-TALENT SURVEY-

As a pastor, and as a church, striving to repair the breaches in the church and community, your talents are essential. Therefore, please complete the survey below, by placing **a check in front of the items** that identify your talent(s). Please also indicate your availability. If your talents are not listed, please add them. Thank you.

Name_____

Telephone ( )_____

Address _____

    (Number)   (Street)

_____

    (City)   (Zip Code)

WHAT ARE YOUR TALENTS?

   _____ **Musical**

   _____ **Singing**

   _____ **Playing Musical Instruments (Which One?)**

_____

_____ *Academic*

   _____ **Clerical**

   _____ **Accounting**

   _____ **Bookkeeping**

   _____ **Proposal Writing**

_____ *Mentoring*

   _____ **Boys**

   _____ **Girls**

_____ *Media Production*

   _____ **Audio Tapes**

   _____ **Video Tapes**

   _____ **Photography**

   _____ **Film**

   _____ **Sound Technician**

_____ *Fitness*

   _____ **Aerobics**

   _____ **Dancing**

   _____ **Nutrition**

_____ *Technology*

   _____ **Computers**

   _____ **Web Paging**

_____ *Evangelizing*

   _____ **Witnessing**

   _____ **Teaching**

   _____ **Would You**

   _____ **If We Trained You?**

Teach

_____ *Tutoring*

    _____ English

    _____ Mathematics

    _____ Reading

Page 2. Talent Cont'd.

_____*Trades*

    _____ Carpentry

    _____ Cooking

    _____ Cosmetology

    _____ Drama

    _____ Decorating

    _____ Landscaping

    _____Mechanically   Inclined

(How)_____

_____ *Public Relations*

    _____ Greeting People

    _____ Working with Children

    _____ Working With Teenagers

_____ *Sports*

    _____ Baseball

    _____ Basketball

    _____ Volleyball

    _____ Softball

    _____ Wrestling

Hobbies

_____

_____

ADD ANY TALENTS NOT LISTED -

_____

_____

_____

_____

_____

_____

_____

_____

_____

_____

HOW MUCH TIME ARE YOU WLLING TO VOLUNTEER PER WEEK_____

WHAT WEEK (s) ARE YOU AVAILABLE:
lst _____ 2nd _____ 3rd_____ 4th _____

WHAT DAY (S) OF THE WEEK ARE YOU AVAILABLE:
Monday ____
Tuesday ____
Wednesday ____
Thursday ____
Friday ____
Saturday ____

WHAT TIME ARE YOU AVAILABLE: _____

Appendix F: Ministry Sign-Up

St. Paul Missionary Baptist Church

6954 South Union Avenue Chicago, IL 60621
REVEREND JOEL D. TAYLOR, Pastor

MINISTRY SIGN-UP

As pastor, I would like to express my appreciation to each of you for responding to the <u>Talent Survey</u> conducted on Sunday, October 19, 1997. The purpose of the survey was to identify talent(s) here in St. Paul, which are essential as we go forward to repair the breaches. The talents listed below will begin our ministries. Other ministries will be added in the future. Accordingly, please place a check by the talent(s), which you are ready to utilize for ministry. Thank you!

Name _____

Telephone (_____) _____ -_____

Address

_____

    (Number)   **(Street)**

_____

    (City)   **(Zip Code)**

_____*Evangelizing*

        _____**Witnessing**

        _____**Teaching**

_____*Technology*

        _____**Computers**

        _____**Web Paging**

_____*Prayer*

        _____**Prayer & Visitation**

_____*Tutoring*

        _____**English**

        _____**Mathematics**

        _____**Reading**

_____*Fitness*

        _____**Aerobics**

        _____**Dancing**

        _____**Nutrition**

_____*Mentoring*

        _____**Boys**

        _____**Girls**

_____*My Brothers Keeper*

        _____**Counseling Battered Women**

        _____**Feeding**

        _____**Clothing Give-Away**

_____*Athletic*

        _____**Baseball**

        _____**Basketball**

        _____**Volleyball**

        _____**Softball**

        _____**Wrestling**

I am willing to volunteer _____ *day(s) per week: Monday* _____ *Tuesday*
_____ *Wednesday* _____ *Thursday* _____ *Friday* _____ *Saturday* _____

I am willing to serve _____ (minutes ___ hours ___) per day.
  From _____ AM/PM to _____ AM/PM

Appendix G: Data Tables

COMPOSITES OF RESPONSES TO MEMBERSHIP SURVEY
SOCIAL ACTIVISM
8/31/97 & 9/7/97

I   SOCIAL   BACKGROUND   NUMBER %
CHARACTERS

1. Sex			
	Male	30	15.6%
	Female	63	32.8%
	Unknown	99	51.6%
		192	100.0%

2. Age			
	12 - 18	27	14.1%
	19 - 35	60	31.3%
	36 - 49	43	22.4%
	50 - 65	47	24.5%
	66 - Up	11	5.7%
	Unknown	4	2.1%
		192	100.0%

II Mission Opportunity Responses
1. Believe they are active in social concerns of the community.

	Number	%
Yes	117	60.9%
No	66	34.4%
Unknown	9	4.7%
	192	100.0%

2. Live in the Englewood Community.

	Number	%
Yes	59	30.7%
No	129	67.2%
Unknown	4	2.1%
	192	100.0%

3. The responsibility to teach young people what they should be taught in the public school system should be taught by the church.

	Number	%
Strongly Disagree	13	6.8%
Disagree	29	15.1%
Undecided	30	15.6%
Agree	61	31.8%
Strongly Agree	53	27.6%
Unknown	6	3.1%
	192	100.0%

4. Part of the mission of the church is to teach young people biblical principals.

	Number	%
Strongly Disagree	18	9.4%
Disagree	4	2.1%
Undecided	3	1.6%
Agree	35	18.2%
Strongly Agree	128	66.7%
Unknown	4	2.1%
	192	100.0%

5. Men of the church should take an interest in young people and help them develop into Moral & Spiritual people.

	Number	%
Strongly Disagree	15	7.8%
Disagree	6	3.1%
Undecided	6	3.1%
Agree	34	17.7%
Strongly Agree	126	65.6%
Unknown	5	2.6%
	192	100.0%

6. Young mothers can benefit from the experiences of older more mature women of the church.

	Number	%
Strongly Disagree	14	7.3%
Disagree	4	2.1%
Undecided	12	6.3%
Agree	41	21.4%
Strongly Agree	79	41.1%
Unknown	42	21.9%
	192	100.0%

7. Morals and values should be taught through the activities in the church.

	Number	%
Strongly Disagree	10	5.2%
Disagree	10	5.2%
Undecided	5	2.6%
Agree	60	31.3%
Strongly Agree	103	53.6%
Unknown	4	2.1%
	192	100.0%

8. The Church should be concerned about preparing our young people to get a job.

	Number	%

Strongly Disagree	15	7.8%
Disagree	6	3.1%
Undecided	21	10.9%
Agree	55	28.6%
Strongly Agree	91	47.4%
Unknown	4	2.1%
	192	100.0%

9. The Church should be concerned about social issues related to young people.

	Number	%
Strongly Disagree	13	6.8%
Disagree	8	4.2%
Undecided	14	7.3%
Agree	51	26.6%
Strongly Agree	102	53.1%
Unknown	4	2.1%
	192	100.0%

10. The church should have recreational activities.

	Number	%
Strongly Disagree	12	6.3%
Disagree	2	1.0%
Undecided	5	2.6%
Agree	67	34.9%
Strongly Agree	100	52.1%
Unknown	6	3.1%
	192	100.0%

11. An area in the building should be used for social as well as academic activities.

	Number	%
Strongly Disagree	10	5.2%
Disagree	9	4.7%
Undecided	14	7.3%
Agree	68	35.4%
Strongly Agree	87	45.3%
Unknown	4	2.1%

12. Our teens should receive social, as well as academic counseling.

	Number	%
Strongly Disagree	12	6.3%
Disagree	9	4.7%
Undecided	4	2.1%
Agree	66	34.4%
Strongly Agree	86	44.8%
Unknown	15	7.8%
	192	100.0%

13. Willing to participate in ministries to address issues concerning my community.

	Number	%
Strongly Disagree	9	4.7%
Disagree	6	3.1%
Undecided	18	9.4%
Agree	76	39.6%
Strongly Agree	67	34.9%
Unknown	16	8.3%
	192	100.0%

14. Willing to participate in seminars and training sessions to prepare for participation in these ministries.

	Number	%
Strongly Disagree	10	5.2%
Disagree	6	3.1%
Undecided	22	11.5%
Agree	70	36.5%
Strongly Agree	65	33.9%
Unknown	19	9.9%
	192	100.0%

15. The church should help educate our youth in the church and community with tutoring services.

	Number	%
Strongly Disagree	10	5.2%
Disagree	3	1.6%
Undecided	6	3.1%
Agree	63	32.8%
Strongly Agree	94	49.0%
Unknown	16	8.3%
	192	100.0%

16. The church should be concerned about people accepting the Lord as their personal savior and forget about social, economic and family issues.

	Number	%
Strongly Disagree	49	25.5%
Disagree	38	19.8%
Undecided	14	7.3%
Agree	25	13.0%
Strongly Agree	49	25.5%
Unknown	17	8.9%
	192	100.0%

17. Preaching can change my attitude on any of these statements.

	Number	%
Strongly Disagree	17	8.9%
Disagree	15	7.8%
Undecided	28	14.6%
Agree	61	31.8%
Strongly Agree	53	27.6%
Unknown	18	9.4%
	192	100.0%

18. Sermons I hear can motivate me to play a key part regarding social activism.

	Number	%
Strongly Disagree	11	5.7%
Disagree	6	3.1%
Undecided	17	8.9%
Agree	65	33.9%
Strongly Agree	73	38.0%
Unknown	20	10.4%
	192	100.0%

19. How much time I am willing to volunteer per week to improve social activism at our church.

	Number	%
Thirty Minutes	15	7.8%
One Hour	76	39.6%
Two Hours	77	40.1%
No Time At All	4	2.1%
Unknown	20	10.4%
	192	100.0%

COMPOSITES OF RESPONSES TO SECOND MEMBERSHIP
SURVEY
SOCIAL ACTIVISM - OCTOBER 26TH &
NOVEMBER 2, 1997

I SOCIAL BACKGROUND CHARACTERS

		NUMBER	%
1. Sex	Male	24	15.7%
	Female	67	43.8%
	Unknown	62	40.5%
		153	100.0%
2. Age	12 - 18	14	9.2%
	19 - 35	64	41.8%
	36 - 49	37	24.2%
	50 - 65	25	16.3%
	66 - Up	10	6.5%
	Unknown	3	2.0%
		153	100.0%

II Mission Opportunity Responses

1. Believe they are active in social concerns of the community.

	Number	%
Yes	105	68.6%
No	35	22.9%
Unknown	13	8.5%
	153	100.0%

2. Live in the Englewood Community	Number	%
Yes	74	48.4%
No	73	47.7%
Unknown	6	3.9%
	153	100.0%

3. The responsibility to teach young people what they should be taught in the public school system should be taught by the church.

	Number	%
Strongly Disagree	5	3.3%
Disagree	22	14.4%
Undecided	13	8.5%
Agree	53	34.6%
Strongly Agree	58	37.9%
Unknown	2	1.3%
	153	100.0%

4. Part of the mission of the church is to teach young people biblical principles.

	Number	%
Strongly Disagree	3	2.0%
Disagree	1	0.7%
Undecided	2	1.3%
Agree	34	22.2%
Strongly Agree	113	73.9%
Unknown	0	0.0%
	153	100.0%

5. Men of the church should take an interest in young people and help them develop into Moral & Spiritual people.

	Number	%
Strongly Disagree	4	2.6%
Disagree	2	1.3%
Undecided	4	2.6%
Agree	37	24.2%
Strongly Agree	106	69.3%
Unknown	0	0.0%
	153	100.0%

6. Young mothers can benefit from the experiences of older more mature women of the church.

	Number	%
Strongly Disagree	2	1.3%
Disagree	1	0.7%
Undecided	3	2.0%
Agree	43	28.1%

	Number	%
Strongly Agree	102	66.7%
Unknown	2	1.3%
	153	100.0%

7. Morals and values should be taught through the activities in the church.

	Number	%
Strongly Disagree	5	3.3%
Disagree	1	0.7%
Undecided	15	9.8%
Agree	40	26.1%
Strongly Agree	92	60.1%
Unknown	0	0.0%
	153	100.0%

8. The Church should be concerned about preparing our young people to get a job.

	Number	%
Strongly Disagree	4	2.6%
Disagree	4	2.6%
Undecided	6	3.9%
Agree	58	37.9%
Strongly Agree	79	51.6%
Unknown	2	1.3%
	153	100.0%

9. The Church should be concerned about social issues related to young people.

	Number	%
Strongly Disagree	2	1.3%
Disagree	2	1.3%
Undecided	6	3.9%
Agree	53	34.6%
Strongly Agree	90	58.8%
Unknown	0	0.0%
	153	100.0%

10. The church should have recreational activities.

	Number	%

Strongly Disagree	3	2.0%
Disagree	1	0.7%
Undecided	4	2.6%
Agree	50	32.7%
Strongly Agree	94	61.4%
Unknown	1	0.7%
	153	100.0%

11. An area in the building should be used for social as well as academic activities.

	Number	%
Strongly Disagree	1	0.7%
Disagree	2	1.3%
Undecided	9	5.9%
Agree	63	41.2%
Strongly Agree	76	49.7%
Unknown	2	1.3%
	153	100.0%

12. Our teens should receive social, as well as academic counseling.

	Number	%
Strongly Disagree	1	0.7%
Disagree	1	0.7%
Undecided	4	2.6%
Agree	52	34.0%
Strongly Agree	95	62.1%
Unknown	0	0.0%
	153	100.0%

13. Willing to participate in ministries to address issues concerning my community.

	Number	%
Strongly Disagree	1	0.7%
Disagree	1	0.7%
Undecided	10	6.5%
Agree	69	45.1%

Strongly Agree	70	45.8%
Unknown	2	1.3%
	153	100.0%

14. Willing to participate in seminars and training sessions to prepare for participation in these ministries.

	Number	%
Strongly Disagree	3	2.0%
Disagree	1	0.7%
Undecided	12	7.8%
Agree	66	43.1%
Strongly Agree	69	45.1%
Unknown	2	1.3%
	153	100.0%

15. The church should help educate our youth in the church and community with tutoring services.

	Number	%
Strongly Disagree	3	2.0%
Disagree	1	0.7%
Undecided	2	1.3%
Agree	48	31.4%
Strongly Agree	97	63.4%
Unknown	2	1.3%
	153	100.0%

16. The church should be concerned about people accepting the Lord as their personal savior and forget about social, economic and family issues.

	Number	%
Strongly Disagree	24	15.7%
Disagree	27	17.6%
Undecided	12	7.8%
Agree	33	21.6%
Strongly Agree	54	35.3%
Unknown	3	2.0%
	153	100.0%

17. Preaching can change my attitude on any of these statements.

	Number	%
Strongly Disagree	18	11.8%
Disagree	14	9.2%
Undecided	22	14.4%
Agree	50	32.7%
Strongly Agree	44	28.8%
Unknown	5	3.3%
	153	100.0%

18. Sermons I hear can motivate me to play a key part regarding social activism.

	Number	%
Strongly Disagree	3	2.0%
Disagree	7	4.6%
Undecided	10	6.5%
Agree	62	40.5%
Strongly Agree	69	45.1%
Unknown	2	1.3%
	153	100.0%

19. How much time I am willing to volunteer per week to improve social activism at our church.

	Number	%
Thirty Minutes	11	7.2%
One Hour	33	21.6%
Two Hours	98	64.1%
No Time At All	2	1.3%
Unknown	9	5.9%
	153	100.0%

PERCENTAGE OF CHANGE BETWEEN PRE- AND POST-TEST
SOCIAL ACTIVISM
8/31/97 & 9/7/97

I SOCIAL BACKGROUND CHARACTERS		Pre-test	Post-test	Change
1. Sex	Male	15.6%	15.7%	0.1%
	Female	32.8%	43.8%	11.0%

	Unknown	51.6%	40.5%	-11.1%
		100.0%	100.0%	

2. Age	12 - 18	14.1%	9.2%	-4.9%
	19 - 35	31.2%	41.8%	10.6%
	36 - 49	22.4%	24.2%	1.8%
	50 - 65	24.5%	16.3%	-8.2%
	66 - Up	5.7%	6.5%	0.8%
	Unknown	2.1%	2.0%	-0.1%
		100.0%	100.0%	

II Mission Opportunity Responses

1. Believe they are active in social concerns of the community.

	Number	%	Change
Yes	60.9%	68.6%	7.7%
No	34.4%	22.9%	-11.5%
Unknown	4.7%	8.5%	3.8%
	100.0%	100.0%	

2. Live in the Englewood Community

	Number	%	Change
Yes	30.7%	48.4%	17.7%
No	67.2%	47.7%	-19.5%
Unknown	2.1%	3.9%	1.8%
	100.0%	100.0%	

3. The responsibility to teach young people what they should be taught in the public school system should be taught by the church.

	Number	%	Change
Strongly Disagree	6.8%	3.3%	-3.5%
Disagree	15.1%	14.4%	-0.7%
Undecided	15.6%	8.5%	-7.1%
Agree	31.8%	34.6%	2.8%
Strongly Agree	27.6%	37.9%	10.3%
Unknown	3.1%	1.3%	-1.8%
	100.0%	100.0%	

4. Part of the mission of the church is to teach

young people biblical principles.

	Number	%	Change
Strongly Disagree	9.4%	2.0%	-7.4%
Disagree	2.1%	0.7%	-1.4%
Undecided	1.6%	1.3%	-0.3%
Agree	18.2%	22.2%	4.0%
Strongly Agree	66.7%	73.9%	7.2%
Unknown	2.0%	0.0%	-2.0%
	100.0%	100.1%	

5. Men of the church should take an interest in young people and help them develop into Moral & Spiritual people.

	Number	%	Change
Strongly Disagree	7.8%	2.6%	-5.2%
Disagree	3.1%	1.3%	-1.8%
Undecided	3.1%	2.6%	-0.5%
Agree	17.8%	24.2%	6.4%
Strongly Agree	65.6%	69.3%	3.7%
Unknown	2.6%	0.0%	-2.6%
	100.0%	100.0%	

6. Young mothers can benefit from the experiences of older more mature women of the church.

	Number	%	Change
Strongly Disagree	7.3%	1.3%	-6.0%
Disagree	2.1%	0.7%	-1.4%
Undecided	6.2%	2.0%	-4.2%
Agree	21.4%	28.1%	6.7%
Strongly Agree	41.1%	66.7%	25.6%
Unknown	21.9%	1.3%	-20.6%
	100.0%	100.0%	

7. Morals and values should be taught through the activities in the church.

	Number	%	Change
Strongly Disagree	5.2%	3.3%	-1.9%
Disagree	5.2%	0.7%	-4.5%
Undecided	2.6%	9.8%	7.2%

Agree	31.3%	26.1%	-5.2%
Strongly Agree	53.6%	60.1%	6.5%
Unknown	2.1%	0.0%	-2.1%
	100.0%	100.0%	

8. The Church should be concerned about preparing our young people to get a job.

	Number	%	Change
Strongly Disagree	7.8%	2.6%	-5.2%
Disagree	3.1%	2.6%	-0.5%
Undecided	10.9%	3.9%	-7.0%
Agree	28.7%	37.9%	9.2%
Strongly Agree	47.4%	51.6%	4.2%
Unknown	2.1%	1.3%	-0.8%
	100.0%	100.0%	

9. The Church should be concerned about social issues related to young people.

	Number	%	Change
Strongly Disagree	6.8%	1.3%	-5.5%
Disagree	4.1%	1.3%	-2.8%
Undecided	7.3%	3.9%	-3.4%
Agree	26.6%	34.6%	8.0%
Strongly Agree	53.1%	58.8%	5.7%
Unknown	2.1%	0.0%	-2.1%
	100.0%	100.0%	

10. The church should have recreational activities.

	Number	%	Change
Strongly Disagree	6.3%	2.0%	-4.3%
Disagree	1.0%	0.7%	-0.3%
Undecided	2.6%	2.6%	0.0%
Agree	34.9%	32.7%	-2.2%
Strongly Agree	52.1%	61.4%	9.3%
Unknown	3.1%	0.7%	-2.4%
	100.0%	100.0%	

11. An area in the building should be used for

social as well as academic activities.

	Number	%	Change
Strongly Disagree	5.2%	0.7%	-4.5%
Disagree	4.7%	1.3%	-3.4%
Undecided	7.3%	5.9%	-1.4%
Agree	35.4%	41.2%	5.8%
Strongly Agree	45.3%	49.7%	4.4%
Unknown	2.1%	1.3%	-0.8%
	100.0%	100.0%	

12. Our teens should receive social, as well as academic counseling.

	Number	%	Change
Strongly Disagree	6.2%	0.7%	-5.5%
Disagree	4.7%	0.7%	-4.0%
Undecided	2.1%	2.6%	0.5%
Agree	34.4%	34.0%	-0.4%
Strongly Agree	44.8%	62.1%	17.3%
Unknown	7.8%	0.0%	-7.8%
	100.0%	100.0%	

13. Willing to participate in ministries to address issues concerning my community.

	Number	%	Change
Strongly Disagree	4.7%	0.7%	-4.0%
Disagree	3.1%	0.7%	-2.4%
Undecided	9.4%	6.5%	-2.9%
Agree	39.6%	45.1%	5.5%
Strongly Agree	34.9%	45.8%	10.9%
Unknown	8.3%	1.3%	-7.0%
	100.0%	100.0%	

14. Willing to participate in seminars and training sessions to prepare for participation in these ministries.

	Number	%	Change
Strongly Disagree	5.2%	2.0%	-3.2%
Disagree	3.1%	0.7%	-2.4%
Undecided	11.4%	7.8%	-3.6%
Agree	36.5%	43.1%	6.6%

Strongly Agree	33.9%	45.1%	11.2%
Unknown	9.9%	1.3%	-8.6%
	100.0%	100.0%	

15. The church should help educate our youth in the church and community with tutoring services.

	Number	%	Change
Strongly Disagree	5.2%	2.0%	-3.2%
Disagree	1.6%	0.7%	-0.9%
Undecided	3.1%	1.3%	-1.8%
Agree	32.8%	31.4%	-1.4%
Strongly Agree	49.0%	63.4%	14.4%
Unknown	8.3%	1.3%	-7.0%
	100.0%	100.0%	

16. The church should be concerned about people accepting the Lord as their personal savior and forget about social, economic and family issues.

	Number	%	Change
Strongly Disagree	25.5%	15.7%	-9.8%
Disagree	19.8%	17.6%	-2.2%
Undecided	7.3%	7.8%	0.5%
Agree	13.0%	21.6%	8.6%
Strongly Agree	25.5%	35.3%	9.8%
Unknown	8.9%	2.0%	-6.9%
	100.0%	100.0%	

17. Preaching can change my attitude on any of these statements.

	Number	%	Change
Strongly Disagree	8.8%	11.8%	3.0%
Disagree	7.8%	9.2%	1.4%
Undecided	14.6%	14.4%	-0.2%
Agree	31.8%	32.7%	0.9%
Strongly Agree	27.6%	28.8%	1.2%
Unknown	9.4%	3.3%	-6.1%
	100.0%	100.0%	

18. Sermons I hear can motivate me to play a key part regarding social activism.

	Number	%	Change
Strongly Disagree	5.7%	2.0%	-3.7%
Disagree	3.1%	4.6%	1.5%
Undecided	8.9%	6.5%	-2.4%
Agree	33.9%	40.5%	6.6%
Strongly Agree	38.0%	45.1%	7.1%
Unknown	10.4%	1.3%	-9.1%
	100.0%	100.0%	

19. How much time I am willing to volunteer per week to   improve social activism at our church.

	Number	%	Change
Thirty Minutes	7.8%	7.2%	-0.6%
One Hour	39.6%	21.6%	-18.0%
Two Hours	40.1%	64.1%	24.0%
No Time At All	2.1%	1.3%	-0.8%
Unknown	10.4%	5.9%	-4.5%
	100.0%	100.0%	

About the Author

The Reverend Dr. Joel Damon Taylor is a third generation ordained pastor in the Baptist Church. Since 1985, Dr. Taylor has served as the pastor of St. Paul Missionary Baptist Church in Chicago, where his father, the late Rev. Jasper J. Taylor Sr., served as pastor and in 2004, he accepted the leadership as pastor of the Greater Mount Pleasant Missionary Baptist Church, which was organized and pastored by his father-in-law, the late Rev. J.P. White.

Dr. Taylor represents the new generation of preachers who are intellectually sound, culturally sensitive, prophetically committed, and spiritually anointed. He is a Fitchue McRae Fellow graduate of United Theological Seminary, where he earned his Doctor of Ministry in 1998. Dr. Taylor is a native of the Englewood area of Chicago, a Religious Studies graduate of DePaul University and earned his Master of Divinity degree at Northern Baptist Theological Seminary in Lombard, Illinois. While at Northern Baptist Theological Seminary, the faculty and staff recognized Dr. Taylor as a 'preacher of power.'

Time has proven that Dr. Taylor's ministry is powerful, personal, and progressive. During his tenure as Pastor, Dr. Taylor has led both congregations to become driven and directed by God in their mission, mandate and ministry. He has sought to help God's people understand and live out the five-fold purpose as a body of baptized believers through Worship, Evangelism, Discipleship, Fellowship and Service. In conjunction with the five-fold purpose, Dr. Taylor has developed the Soul Winning Action Team (SWAT), which specializes in crusading in the surrounding community and spreading the good news about the Lord Jesus Christ outside of the church.

Dr. Taylor currently serves as the President of the Illinois National Baptist State Convention, is a member of the Evangelical Board of the National Baptist Convention of America, Inc., and is the Director of the Congress of Discipleship and Christian Education for the National Baptist Convention of America Inc., Int'l. Prior to serving as the Director of the Congress of Discipleship and Christian Education, Dr. Taylor served as the Director of the NBCA Inc., Int'l Youth Convention. In addition, Dr. Taylor is a student mentor and liaison for M.Div and D.Min students at Shaw University affiliated with NBCA Inc., Int'l.

Dr. Taylor serves a great God who is still doing great things. He is married to the former Cynthia Vernice White, who is a wonderful vocalist, a Licensed Professional Health Therapist, and a gift to him from God. They are the proud parents of two children: Rev. Jasper Paul and Jessica Dominique.

About Sermon To Book

SermonToBook.com began with a simple belief: that sermons should be touching lives, *not* collecting dust. That's why we turn sermons into high-quality books that are accessible to people all over the globe.

Turning your sermon series into a book exposes more people to God's Word, better equips you for counseling, accelerates future sermon prep, adds credibility to your ministry, and even helps make ends meet during tight times.

John 21:25 tells us that the world itself couldn't contain the books that would be written about the work of Jesus Christ. Our mission is to try anyway. Because, in Heaven, there will no longer be a need for sermons or books. Our time is now.

If God so leads you, we'd love to work with you on your sermon or sermon series.

Visit www.sermontobook.com to learn more.

Made in the USA
San Bernardino, CA
16 August 2016